SPIRITUAL
FITNESS

SPIRITUAL
FITNESS

A SEVEN WEEK GUIDE TO FINDING
MEANING AND SACREDNESS
IN YOUR EVERYDAY LIFE

CAROLINE REYNOLDS

Thorsons

Thorsons
An Imprint of HarperCollins*Publishers*
77–85 Fulham Palace Road,
Hammersmith, London W6 8JB

The Thorsons website address is: www.thorsons.com

First published by Thorsons 2001

1 3 5 7 9 10 8 6 4 2

A catalogue record of this book is
available from the British Library

ISBN 0 00 710666 1

Printed and bound in Great Britain by
Martins the Printers Ltd, Berwick-upon-Tweed

CONTENTS

Introduction   xi

1   Motivation Recharge   1

2   Soul Detox   19

3   Minding Your Language   46

4   The Relationship Equation   68

5   Learning to Meditate   91

6   Taking the Leap & Finding Your Purpose   118

7   Holding Your Power & Living with Joy   142

Afterword   162

About the Author   164

Index   165

To my parents, Joy and Brian,
for teaching me the meaning of real kindness

ACKNOWLEDGEMENTS

Spiritual Fitness is the result of all my experiences, encounters and relationships so far. Therefore I would like to thank all the people who have come into my life at various times for the soul gifts they have offered me in my understanding of life. Specifically I would like to acknowledge all those who have helped me directly with this book. My deepest thanks go to Denise Linn, for seeing my light before I could and constantly encouraging me; Malka Golden-Wolfe, for leading me to my strength; my parents, Brian and Joy, for their unconditional support, and my sister, Celia, for so enthusiastically reviewing my script. Also my dear friend Cristen Francis for her constant encouragement, and Maria Kitsis and Dana Morgan at Destiny in Radlett, for supporting my work so well.

Thanks also to Carole Tonkinson, Ariel Kahn, Karen Kreiger and everyone at Thorsons who has guided me through this project; Jan Gardener at Paths of Wisdom, St Albans and Eileen Campbell for her bold intuition in getting me started, and Matthew Cory for his sensitive editing. During the writing of this book, I have also received great support from my friends in Sedona, Arizona, especially my guiding light, Anne Emerson, Nell Shively and Joni Shuman, Ed and Kris Varjean at The Lantern Light Inn, Pat Fontan and Gerre Grande at Fango, the Sundance family – Wildflower, Elk, Dreamer and Rain Cloud, and Joanna Giles. And thanks to those who read through the early drafts, Cheryl Van Blerk and Deborah Smith of Pansy Productions, Alison Atwell, Michele Knight, Pam Robinson, Kim and Dick Rae, Samantha Russell, Roger and Ros at Pathway Designs, Shari Carr and Amber Dotts.

Finally special thanks go to all those of you who have attended my Spiritual Fitness WorkOut Groups and other events, who have shared in my growth and allowed me to explore and expand the concepts you will find in this course.

INTRODUCTION

**'And the day came when the risk it took to remain
tight in the bud was more painful than
the risk it took to blossom.'**

Anais Nin

WHAT IS SPIRITUAL FITNESS?

Do you know anyone who is perfect? Do you know anyone who
is so spiritual they never have any emotional, health or financial
problems? If so, please tell them to come forward – many people have
been expecting them for 2000 years! For the rest of us, spirituality
is not about being perfect but about *aspiring* to a life of heart-filled
integrity. It is a journey and not a destination. When we are spiritually
fit and balanced we are a powerfully exquisite blend of human falli-
bility and divine perfection. It is this dynamic tension that gives us our
uniqueness, our power to create and our compassion.

So what exactly is Spiritual Fitness and how do you get some? Have
you got what it takes and what can you expect to get out of it? And
after all that, why should you care? Questions, questions, questions!
Life is full of questions, yet as you begin to bring your mind and soul
into their peak condition, you'll find that, in return, life is full of
answers. If you'd like to know just how spiritually fit you are right now,

you can start by asking yourself the following questions. How loving and kind am I? How free am I? How honest am I? How wise am I? How at peace am I? How joyful am I? These qualities are the cornerstones of Spiritual Fitness.

Spiritual Fitness is your natural birthright. It is as natural to us all as our capacity to laugh and cry. Along with our other two most basic needs – the physical need for food and shelter, and the emotional need for love and sex – there is also our much ignored but just as vital spiritual need – the need for faith and meaning. We all need to believe in something. We all have an innate yearning to find a purpose to our lives, to connect with a higher power and to feel part of the world around us. We long to be able to trust again, to live in peace, with tenderness, creativity, hope and courage. We want to feel the true meaning of love and happiness.

For me, the overwhelming need to get spiritually fit came when I was forced to face an agonizing sense of emptiness inside me, after I had spent years moving away from my natural innocence and sense of spiritual connection. I had come to feel so spiritually bereft that I believed that I could only connect with others intimately through alcohol and sex. Despite the apparent rawness of these two states, they provided me with a veil behind which I could hide my sensitive, soul-searching nature. I eventually came to realize that the closeness I craved with others could not automatically be provided by lying in someone's arms – more often than not I was literally 'lying' in their arms! When chronic ill health catapulted me into a radical lifestyle change, I began to attend workshops that forced me to be open with others in an authentic, everyday way that I hadn't experienced since early childhood. I came out of hiding and the real love that I started to feel melted my frozen heart and taught me how to connect with others on a healthy, genuinely intimate soul level.

When we are spiritually unfit, we spend our lives aching to be real because we have forgotten how to be authentic. We take part of ourselves to work, bring home another part to our relationships and keep another part safely hidden away to do our secret dreaming for us. We live our lives pretending we are small and inconsequential when in fact we are each engaged on an epic journey. Only when you can see the greater significance to all of the events of your life can you find real fulfilment. For example, you might come to realize that the bills you have to pay are actually invitations to you to create a flow of money out of your own talents and faith. You can either spend your time hoping for a wage increase or you can allow your true resources to open up your creativity, remind you who you came here to be and then joyously and passionately make your unique contribution to life.

Spiritual Fitness is not about *what you do*, (although there are plenty of practical exercises here to help keep you spiritually attuned), but about *who you are* in your day-to-day dealings. That means you can read all the right books, wear all the right clothes, and have all the right guides, but if you don't know how to feel real love in your heart, bring a smile to the face of everyone you meet and ease the tears of a child, you're not yet ready to ascend or call yourself a spiritual master. When you are spiritually fit you radiate the warmth and depth of truth, love and wisdom.

Like physical fitness, Spiritual Fitness involves desire, dedication and discipline – one day of exercise is not enough to keep you fit for the rest of the year. Reading a few books, meditating occasionally or attending the odd, and sometimes very odd, workshop will not set you up for the rest of your life. It is an everyday journey that never ends, forever revealing a deeper awareness of how to understand your life. This awareness makes you more sensitive and demands your constant vigilance. Like every other development, it also takes practice.

When you're in good spiritual shape, you are far better able to withstand and overcome life's vicissitudes and create the lifestyle that best suits who you truly are in everything from relationships and finances to career and creativity. In the process, you also eliminate a truck load of stress from your life. As your mind lets go of obsessive worrying by trusting in the guidance of a higher power, you free up a lot of brain and heart space that can be filled with creativity and love. You'll gradually move to a place in your life where you will trust enough to allow situations to flow along their natural course for your highest good. This is when your dreams will start to come true with an amazing regularity.

WHY WE NEED SPIRITUAL FITNESS

I came up with the term 'Spiritual Fitness' to describe our intense need for peace and sustenance in this fast-track world we have created. We live in constant overwhelm amidst a continuous bombardment of technology and 24 hour living – images, sounds, even tastes and smells are hurled at us with reckless abandon. There are 24-hour supermarkets, 24-hour TV, 24-hour banking and the timeless world of the Internet, all ensuring that insomnia is no longer for loners. Magazines feed on our guilt about our openness to new trends and styles. If you don't feel drawn to the latest fashions/music/faces, then just how alive are you? Every technology manufacturer offers today's upgraded version of yesterday's equipment. Everywhere the emphasis is on focusing externally and measuring up at top speed. Haste is of the essence and we find ourselves racing and chasing after the holy grail of modernity. Yet what have we done to allow our inner mechanism to catch up with these outer changes?

In recent years I have been running weekly Spiritual Fitness WorkOut Groups. We gather together for recognition and support on how we can fulfil our spiritual needs in our everyday lives. I believe the popularity of these groups demonstrates that many of us no longer have a recognized place in which to develop our spiritual awareness. We have no place to explore the sacredness of life. Where Sundays (or the Sabbath) were once reserved for people to rest and develop the spiritual aspect of their being, nowadays most of us have less means or time to be still and acknowledge our infinite selves. This means the responsibility is left increasingly up to you. If you want to expand your inner awareness, you need to spend some quiet solitary time each day connecting with your higher power and for the rest of the time, find as many like-minded souls as you can for mutual encouragement.

Spiritual Fitness is a practical way of living that offers an alternative to the void left in our society by the widespread demise of traditional worship, reverence and charity. It offers instead meditation, respectful awareness and loving kindness. It is also a way for you to reclaim an awareness of the magnitude of your soul's journey through life.

Why I Began to Get Spiritually Fit

For me, rediscovering this awareness was a life-transforming experience. I had spent much of my twenties imagining I was having the time of my life. It was the eighties and the 'greed is good' mentality ensured we had an abundance of everything that was good and bad for us. By the end of the eighties, (and my twenties), I had, in one form or another, three relationships on the go, along with a frantic night and day job in a celebrated London nightclub. I lived in an unreal twilight world of shoulder pads and champagne.

On top of this, or rather underneath it all, I was hauling around a broken heart from the first of my relationships and I was so stressed out by my tangled emotional commitments and my night and day job that sometimes I would literally be 'seeing stars'. Within two years of this insanity, I managed to have a breakdown and contract chronic ulcerative colitis. I took off home to Wales and began to confront the fact that maybe I wasn't as much in charge of my life as I had thought.

My live-in partner had just spent a week at the spiritual centre in Findhorn and came down to teach me how to meditate as the solution to my problems. To this I indignantly responded, 'I have *real* problems to think about and you expect me to sit here and meditate!' At this stage, I didn't realize that my inner self hadn't caught up with my hectic, up-till-dawn outer self. I was soon forced to take a deeper look at the way I lived my life.

I looked around at the world we live in and saw the thousands of machines we have created to do many of our physical and mental chores – yet instead of enjoying all the spare time they have freed up, we get stressed because we can't cram in all the activities that even more technology has provided. So many of us race about in our cars from our computer-based jobs to exercise in the gym, or watch one of the hundreds of available TV channels, spend hours in cyberspace or on our mobile phones. Instead, we could have taken a gentle stroll through the park and looked up at the beauty and mystery of real space above us. It seems we are all in overdrive and are unable to slow down. We have become stimulus junkies.

Rediscovering Our Natural State

What we have forgotten is that life wasn't always like this. It is not our natural state. There was a time when life presented us with ample opportunity for reflection and digestion. Leisure time was not an excuse for mindless activity involving the TV, video games or other gadget-induced oblivion, but it was a time for the creative contemplation of one's life.

I was clearly reminded of this when I spent an afternoon of old-fashioned bucolic charm sitting in the late summer sun with my parents in their Welsh garden. Although I sat diligently attempting to read a book on multi-dimensional cosmic realities, I soon found myself becoming completely absorbed by the very real multi-dimensional level of my parent's conversation and world. While I struggled with who I was, why I was here and which key I should use to unlock my intergalactic identity, their conversation merrily flitted from a discussion on the neighbour's curtains to 'What is the sun?' (At this point they turned hopefully to me. I in turn hid behind my book muttering that it was 'gas'). A brief remark on the state of the monarchy was quickly followed by a query about the number of apples on the garden tree. I soon realized that they had maintained a detached but curious air of contemplative reflection towards the world around them. Most importantly, I saw the peace this attitude produced.

In the meantime, I was there to recuperate from a stress-induced debilitation – I had so many food allergies that I felt as if I could only consume air and water with any safety. My parents in turn heartily ate whatever they liked. I soon began to wonder if I was somehow missing the point! When I looked a little deeper, I understood that contemplation and simplicity are two of the essential components of inner peace. They enable us to slow down and appreciate the meaning and the message of each moment, an essential part of spiritual awareness.

When you slow down you have time to experience the natural ebb and flow of life inside you. Native cultures and our own ancestors knew this state as the circle of life. From the Wiccan Wheel to the Medicine Wheel, birth, death and rebirth were seen as being as natural within ourselves as they are in the cyclical aspects of nature. Each night we have an ebb of about eight hours when we sleep, before the flow of being 'reborn' in the morning. As everything is a microcosm of the macrocosm, so it is through life. For all of us there are periods of thrust, drive and creativity and other times when we feel completely exhausted and disinterested in our own lives.

This doesn't mean that we are failures, losers or out of touch with the modern world. It is important that we come to re-associate these times of apparent sloth and see them for what they really are – times for us to gather ourselves and prepare for the next step up. This is a very natural process of action–assimilation–action. As with physical fitness, it is during the periods following exercise that our 'spiritual muscles' actually grow. Let's once more realize it's OK to stop and rest and allow life's teachings to sink in and strengthen us.

In this century we are moving from the Information Age to the Intuition Age. This means that we should focus less on logical, linear, mechanical thinking and more on creative, lateral and emotional thinking. So, the next time you find yourself watching the TV hoping to catch the weather forecast, try looking out of the window instead.

Let the sky, trees and birds speak to you. It is time for you to 'feel' and reconnect with the natural world.

HOW TO BECOME SPIRITUALLY FIT

Spirituality is a natural and basic human function but, as with physical health and strength, it is how we choose to nurture and develop it that marks us out from each other. If you ask some people what spirituality means, they will answer that they don't know because they have no desire to go to church or bow down to a bearded old man in the sky. If you ask others, they will tell you that they have already met this need by following a particular guru, diet or fairy trail. The spiritual practice of which I am speaking is a million miles away from all of these answers.

The Importance of Kindness

I have two wonderful friends who live in a town in the USA that is known for its high 'spiritual' level of awareness and attendant paraphernalia. My friends have absolutely no interest in any of this and yet they have frequently behaved as no less than angels to me and to many who come into contact with them. They understand one of the basic truths of spirituality – that we are here to be of service and to help each other as much as we can. Once, asked by a member of the community what type of spirituality they practised, they replied in all honesty, 'kindness'. For me this is what spirituality is all about. If you prefer, you can replace the word 'kindness' with 'love'. I use 'kindness' here as 'love' has become a term often open to much misinterpretation.

So if 'spirituality' is simply kindness, to others and yourself, the first essential tool you need is not a Bible, bell or beads but a good and open heart. To reach this state, you must strip yourself back to the source, reconnect with your own essential goodness and then seek out the same in others. Your natural kindness will then make you and everyone around you feel good.

Soul Level Thinking

Every time you concern yourself with who said or did what, with how you are going to react, you are stuck in 'earth level' thinking. This is based on your belief that you are merely an isolated ego-driven being who must fend for yourself against an imagined hostile world. It is where you enter the loop of unproductive and obsessive thought patterns.

With soul level thinking you stand back and break out of this loop. You become aware that you and everyone around you are eternal souls on a mutual journey of self-discovery. Like an artist stepping back to view your work in progress, you start to see the bigger picture and find a deeper meaning and relevance to everything. Your reactions are less knee-jerk and you gain far greater control over your state of mind. Life is no longer a series of random joys and mishaps but becomes instead an interactive training ground, constantly offering you the chance to understand and master yourself.

The important thing to know about soul level thinking is that the soul never makes mistakes – only your mind and emotions can be mistaken. Your soul, the infinite, all-knowing part of you, can always see the highest purpose and perfection in every situation and it is always guiding you to do the same. Therefore the quickest and most powerful way to change your life is to directly access your soul level thinking.

As you strengthen and expand your inner awareness through soul level thinking, you'll find the world around you falling over itself to help you forward. You will realize that every day the universe is constantly offering you clues to your true nature and your path ahead.

HOW THIS COURSE WORKS

This course takes the form of seven weekly WorkOuts that follow a steady progression to expand your awareness and guide you to Spiritual Fitness. Each WorkOut ends with exercises that will help you to put into practice the principles you have just read about. They have been designed to access you on many levels and you'll find that some techniques will work better for you than others. I have included a large cross-section to appeal to all learning styles.

You may want to read the course through first and then come back to the exercises on a weekly basis or you may prefer to read one WorkOut a week. Whichever way you choose, your path to spiritual re-awakening will undoubtedly take you more than seven weeks. It can often take people up to a few years to clear and heal themselves and truly embark on a new and uplifting life. Also, you may learn some aspects more quickly than others. Yet by following this course you will have all the basic tools you need and as you encounter each new stage in your life, you'll be able to return to the relevant WorkOut for a refresher. The WorkOuts progress as follows:

WorkOut One: Motivation Recharge introduces basic motivation skills to give you the momentum to launch yourself on this course.

WorkOut Two: Soul Detox shows you how to detox your soul from all the negative influences that you have accumulated over your lifetime.

WorkOut Three: Minding Your Language provides you with the opportunity to examine your language, see how powerful it is and how you can learn to use it to your maximum benefit.

WorkOut Four: The Relationship Equation guides you through the potential pitfalls of relationships and shows how you can overcome these to create and enjoy healthy, loving connections with others.

WorkOut Five: Learning to Meditate describes different ways of meditating and shows you how to discover the one that is right for you.

WorkOut Six: Taking the Leap & Finding Your Purpose gives practical advice on how to deal with the changes that will take place in your life as you enter onto a path of spiritual re-awakening.

WorkOut Seven: Holding Your Power & Living with Joy teaches how to maintain your spiritual awareness in everyday life and continue to live with peace and joy.

Throughout the course, you will find references to *A Course in Miracles* (Foundation for Inner Peace, Viking: New York). This book of channelled wisdom has helped me greatly in my understanding of love, fear and forgiveness. While many books, teachers and schools of thought have influenced me, I have chosen to cite only this work directly because its teachings seem to be at the basis of all others.

As you progress through *Spiritual Fitness*, you will find concepts and exercises that stretch you, some of which you may at first find difficult to maintain. I will not pretend that I follow all these precepts myself every minute of the day but I can assure you that when I do my life runs much more smoothly and I reach deeper levels of peace, love, joy and creativity.

If at any time you find yourself becoming too serious and obsessing over whether or not you are getting things right, then be aware that you have lost the plot! True Spiritual Fitness involves a lot of fun and laughter and, even if you find yourself having a crisis of some kind, train yourself to stand back and see the absurdity of it all at the same time. Remember to smile to yourself and relax.

By the end of the course you'll find that many of the tools you needed at the start will no longer be necessary, because you will have developed your inner knowing and connection to a higher power. Just as when we learn to ride a bicycle with stabilizer wheels, to swim with inflated armbands or to speak a new language using a dictionary, once you've learned to master the basic skills of Spiritual Fitness you may find that yesterday's tools become tomorrow's limitations. You are then ready to fly free and become co-creator with the universe of your own destiny. So here is your opportunity to embark on a transformational odyssey of self-discovery through the power of Spiritual Fitness.

MOTIVATION RECHARGE

**'Find out who you are
then do it on purpose.'**

Dolly Parton

To be spiritually fit you need to live a life that is successful in every area. To achieve real inner harmony you need to be at peace with your health, love life, finances and career. *Spiritual Fitness* will help you to enjoy the benefits of the world we live in, while helping you to realize that these material benefits are finite and therefore have no intrinsic value in themselves. It is only when you use them to expand your spiritual awareness and growth that they can truly fulfil you. In the first week of this course, let's look at how you can motivate yourself towards achieving a balanced and spiritually fulfilled life.

OVERCOMING THE OBSTACLES TO SPIRITUAL FITNESS

Fear of the Unknown

The hardest thing about getting going is actually getting going. Before we can get started, we have to find a strong enough reason to get us motivated. Until then we create excuses and distractions and then wonder why we feel a subtle sense of frustration running through our lives. Of course, the thing that holds us in our paralysis is fear. Fear of the unknown and what it might demand from us. Fear of failure. Fear that we might have to let go of our past safe identity and create one that is dangerously new. We believe that no matter what misery or boredom we may have to endure, at least we know who we are within these fearful states. Through them, we can count on the familiarity of our actions and reactions, and this reassuring familiarity is our imagined saviour. As the American family therapist Virginia Satir said, 'After survival, familiarity is our most powerful human instinct'.

We fear the unknown more than the known because we think the unknown is unpredictable and that therefore we can't control it. Often, the only way we become motivated is when we have hit rock bottom in one or more areas of our lives. At this point, the pain of remaining stuck in our old patterns finally becomes greater than our fear of stepping out of them into the unknown. When we reach this critical point, where our pain overtakes our fear, we are then dramatically catapulted into new ways of living and being. *A Course In Miracles* tells us that our higher power can only talk to us in language we understand. Therefore, at first most of us must be reached through the language of fear.

In my case, I was reached via a chronic illness that would recur whenever I was getting too attached to a lifestyle that was destructive to my soul. It was the universe's way of pointing out to me that there was an easier way, although at the time this 'wake-up call' always felt more like a death knell! One of my old patterns was that for the best part of 25 years, from my early adulthood, I had spent a lot of my time in an intoxicated haze. As I coped with my external reality by floating above it on a sea of alcohol, the buried aching truth of who I really was would often surface as bravado, frustrated vitriol or helpless tears. Of course, this also resulted in many unfulfilling relationships.

Finally, the universal intelligence had to intervene when I blindly refused to see that there was a less painful way for me to experience life. It was not until my mind started careering out of control to such an extent that I experienced bouts of colitis incontinence that I decided that it might be time to do something different. I finally surrendered my fearful grasp on my familiar but illusory external reality and agreed to exchange it for one that was authentic and truly fulfilling. I was ready to listen.

Dramatic illness, divorce and financial ruin are frequently the tools that the universal intelligence has to use to get our attention before we are prepared to act. If we look back we can see that far gentler options were presented to us earlier, but these held little allure when compared to the familiar reassurance of our fearful thinking. I'm sure you can think of times when you were first introduced to spiritual awareness long before you decided to incorporate it into your life. How many times did someone suggest a book or tape to help inspire you, or invite you to a personal growth course, only for you to dismiss them as a load of nonsense? Now, a few enlightened years later, you might find yourself making the same recommendations to others from on high in your lotus position!

Of course, it is also possible for us to be motivated by desire rather than devastation. The classic example of this is when we fall in love. When our hearts are first blown wide open by romantic love, we are suddenly prepared to consider lifestyle changes that we would previously have rejected. For example, have you ever found yourself taking up a new sport, engaging in a new hobby or just going window-shopping for the pleasure of spending more time with your partner? You might also have found yourself trying new foods, watching different movies or listening to previously unthinkable music! Passion is a powerful force to blast us out of our entrenched ways. Parenthood also brings with it a sudden willingness to consider new and better ways of living. When your child is first born you feel that you want to give them the world and you vow to do the best that you can to provide them with it, no matter what the cost.

Sometimes we hold onto our familiar fears because we feel safe with the numbness they provide. If we take no risks and stay in our constricted, closed place of fear then we might avoid some of the challenges that more fearless souls face. But we must also be aware that, at the same time, our numbness prevents us from experiencing the exhilaration and joy of being alive and present in each moment. As you become more spiritually fit, you will find yourself waking up and wanting to take new strides forward in your life. You will have to trust that you will be given all the tools you need as you take each new leap of faith. Remember that a parachute cannot open while you are still standing on the ground. But the moment you make that bold jump out of your old comfort zone your parachute will instantly unfurl and help you to sail along.

The most interesting thing to understand about your motivation is that you are always driven by your emotions and not by your mind. Logical argument and the rational promise of a better life are not enough to lift you out of your comfort zone. If you are overweight, a heavy drinker or a chain smoker, you will understand this. In short, you must either be excited out or terrified out. Then once you have become motivated, through one means or another, your next task is to stay that way.

FEAR OF OUR OWN GREATNESS

So why is it that we often try to return to our small and fearful selves? It is because our greatest fear is the fear of our own greatness. Ultimately, all of our imagined limitations are convenient distractions from what it is we have come here to do, or, more importantly, who it is that we have come here to be.

The twentieth century helped us to buy into what I call the 'earth level' approach of dealing with our limitations by giving us psychotherapy. While we were busy blaming or excusing one another, talking to empty chairs or hitting pillows, we were forever narrowing our focus and field of vision onto the neuroses of our finite selves. Thus we were cleverly deflecting our minds from getting on with our real task. 'Soul level' infinite thinking gives us the freedom to be our magnificent authentic selves. As the world is speeding up, we are waking up and the old ways are proving ineffectual. Once you have used your emotions to give you a kick-start, it is the yearnings and acknowledgments of your limitless soul that will finally set you on a course of steady growth. The only way for someone to become permanently motivated is for them to recognize that they are a divine being, here on a divine mission, and that only this understanding can bring ultimate fulfilment.

I have developed a very simple technique for this that I call the 'pantomime approach'. In the old English theatrical tradition of children's burlesque theatre, the pantomime actors will pretend to ignore a visual fact and shout 'Oh no it isn't!', to which the children in the audience respond 'Oh yes it is!'. When people come to me, hang their heads and proclaim their weaknesses, I respond with 'Oh no you're not!'. If they are prepared to let go of their false limited selves, they clearly know the game is up. At this point in our global evolution, we owe it to ourselves to stop beating around the bush and playing small and instead get on with assuming our greatness.

A man who had become a serious 'course junkie' once showed up at one of my workshops. He proudly declared that he had been to countless courses and that none of them had ever got him to change. As the day progressed, I noticed how he retreated into a foggy haze every time I asked him a direct question about his potential and purpose. Behind his constant answers of 'I don't know yet' his eyes showed a terrified paralysis at the prospect of seizing his power and doing something concrete to improve his everyday life. I suggested to him that he already knew very well what his true purpose was. The real problem for him lay in his pretence that he was incapable of finding it or doing anything about it. He was involved in a very subtle and yet powerful game of double bluff with himself. When he finally realized that the game was up, over the next few months he began to take actions that propelled him towards his true destiny.

So, what exactly is it about our greatness that creates in us such immobilizing fear? One of the reasons that we are afraid to seize the reins of our lives and stand up to be counted is that we think we don't want the responsibility. For example, you might wonder what will happen if other people notice that you truly are so wonderful and magnificent. Will you feel obliged to maintain a certain standard of being? And what if they become envious of you – will you become a target for their own frustrated and unrealized selves? And what if it doesn't last? After all, didn't you hear somewhere that all good things must come to an end?

These are all earth level ways of dealing with a soul level issue. You must start to regard your life on an infinite scale and enjoy magnificence as your natural birthright. So, when other people notice how great you are, make it your aim to inspire them to be the same. If you are wealthy, invite them over to your luxurious home. Be relaxed and happy and make your success an attractive example for them. If you are in a loving relationship, then you and your partner could spend time together with others so that they can see a genuinely caring, healthy partnership.

Trust that as you become more spiritually fit, you'll develop a natural desire and ability to keep on living at this level. When you have tasted the ease and grace of fearless living, your former lifestyle will seem restricted and unappealing. To return to this would be like giving up your colour TV for a black and white set. You just won't want to do it.

If somebody seems envious and attacks you, then you must remember that all attack is only a cry for help. Behind all negative behaviour is fear and as a spiritually fit being your task is to seek out that fear and disarm it. Success can sometimes stir up in others fearful feelings of inadequacy. Learn to ignore meaningless insults and, if the opportunity arises, find a way to help anyone who attacks you to access and realize their own power. (We shall look at how you can do this in later

WorkOuts). If this isn't possible, focus only on your own soul level consciousness and allow those engaged in such earth level concerns to follow you at their own pace. The magnanimity and detachment you will need for this are two of the new resources you will access through your Spiritual Fitness.

And, instead of worrying about how long a good thing lasts, just remember that in the eternal world of the soul nothing comes to an end. All is a cycle of birth, death and rebirth into another form. All you need to do is understand that life is constant motion and that whatever comes next is always going to be a step up for you.

FEAR OF FAILURE

Another fear that holds us back from taking action is our fear of failure. We fear that our disappointment at not succeeding, compounded by the loss of our old familiar world, would be too much of a crushing blow for us to bear. For example, what if you start a new career or a new relationship, or simply adopt a set of new beliefs, and it doesn't work out as you planned? If you look closely at this problem you'll see that it contains its own solution.

The only way you can ever truly fail is if you have a set idea, an expectation of exactly how things should work out. If they turn out differently and you still regard them in this fixed manner, you won't be able to see the unexpected lessons they carry for you. For instance, a failed relationship may tell you more about yourself than years of remaining in frightened solitude could ever have done. Financial hardship can force you to swallow your pride and reach out to others for guidance and support. Every situation holds within it seeds for growth and your life is always enriched by the benefit of experience. To overcome your fear of failure, you need only trust that *any* outcome increases your Spiritual Fitness, regardless of how it may look to you at the time. There can be no such thing as failure if you haven't formed a preconceived idea of what success should look like. Failure is comparative.

Procrastination

After you have overcome your denial of your own greatness and allayed your fears, you have to pass through yet another clever distraction from your journey to Spiritual Fitness. This is the quagmire of procrastination. Most of us have experienced the gnawing ache inside us that says 'I know I should do that', which is closely followed by a pervasive paralysis that replies 'But I think I'll do it next week'. You may know how quickly this syndrome can make you retreat into an unproductive cocoon of familiarity. This means that your subconscious mind is constantly tantalized and then disappointed by the failed prospect of positive action. Every time you make a grand claim such as 'That's it, I have given up drinking/smoking/unhealthy relationships' or 'I'm going to spring-clean the house this weekend' and then don't, you are giving yourself the dangerous signal that you are a liar who is not to be trusted.

I had a friend who repeatedly assured me over the course of a year that she had finished her abusive relationship. Each time she was more and more resolute and each time, within days the relationship was back on again, even though deep down she knew she was just postponing the inevitable break-up. Eventually I stopped giving her advice and taking her seriously. I realized that she was still caught in a loop where she was subconsciously choosing to stay until she could be sure of the lesson she needed to learn – namely, that she was so much bigger than all of this drama. In the same way, if you think of your own highest self as your best friend, constantly having to listen to your broken promises, you will realize how important it is for you to give yourself the message that you are serious and that you mean business.

When you are ready to walk your talk, when you know you can rely on the truth of your own statements, you feel a refreshing sense of reassurance and ease with yourself. (We shall look at this concept in more depth in WorkOut Three). To begin to get yourself motivated, start by making small promises you know you can deliver. As you live up to these promises, you will start to trust yourself more. You will no longer have to tolerate a sheepish sense of guilt or denial about your false promises and instead you will more feel solid and powerful in your life. You will find that once you *get* going, you are more able to *keep* going.

GETTING STARTED

What, Why, How

There are basically two ways to get what you want in life. One is through meditation and divine grace. (This is the fast-track method that we shall look at in Workout Five. But, before you can get there, you'll need the motivation to meditate in the first place.) The other is a simple method to help you get moving and achieve your dreams. It is based on the principle of 'what, why, how'. First of all you need a clear idea of your desired final outcome, then you must have a strong enough reason to move towards it and, finally, you need to come up with concrete steps that you can take immediately to get the ball rolling.

I encountered a clear illustration of the power of this principle when a few years ago I visited Havasupai, an old Native American village inside the Grand Canyon famed for its spectacularly beautiful waterfalls. There is no road into this village, only a narrow trail which winds steeply down the canyon wall and which takes about an hour to walk down. The path then flattens out for the remaining three-hour hike. Congratulating myself on making the journey and feeling more than a little stiff for the next two days, I decided I would leave by helicopter. However, on the eve of my departure, I discovered to my horror that there were no flights out the next day!

The next morning I set off at dawn and spent a blissful three hours walking alone through the magnificent canyon with only the sound of the crackling dry red earth under my feet and the occasional soaring of a bird in the turquoise sky overhead to remind me that I existed. When I arrived at the base of the steep canyon wall I was suddenly overcome by apprehension. Not being in the best physical shape, I wondered how on earth I was going to reach the top. Quite spontaneously I adopted the what, why, how principle to get me to my destination.

First I looked up at the end of the trail far in the distance above me. This gave me a clear goal, something specific to work towards. This was my 'what'. Then I put it out of my sight and instead focused on the steep path in front of me that didn't look at all inviting. I realized that the only way I was going to get up to the top was to be driven by my emotions. I needed to be excited or terrified out. Since it seemed like such a daunting prospect, I decided to go for both! I thought of the 'why', the reasons I wanted to get out of the canyon – there was someone I loved waiting for me and there was also food at the top. And I thought of the reasons I didn't want to stay there – it was getting hot and my only other option was to turn around and walk back for another three hours. Within moments, I had created some very powerful desires to get myself out of there.

My next task was to find a way to climb up the path that would not exhaust me too much. I closed my eyes, prayed and was given the following inner guidance – 'Take ten steps at a time and then stop and look back.' I needed to gather all my energy and focus it on taking small moves, staying in the present moment. This is the only way that we can ever achieve our goals. If I had been continually looking up at my final destination, I would soon have fallen flat on my face. Instead, I had to hold my goal in my heart and allow its presence there to guide me. So many people become overwhelmed at the distance they feel is between their dreams and their current lifestyle. They then use this gulf as a reason not even to bother trying to achieve them. You must start by breaking your dreams down into manageable, bite-size pieces.

By doing this, finally, I reached the top and when I looked back at the vast canyon spread out before me, I had not only an exhilarating sense of achievement but also a deepened faith in the higher power that guides us all.

Recognizing the 'Payoff' Syndrome

Before you can go after what you want, you must first ask yourself why you don't want it. 'But I do want it' I hear you cry, to which I reply 'Then why haven't you got it?' If you are truly and unequivocally driven, there are very few things in this life that you cannot achieve. Yet many of us are seduced by the deceptive appeal of the 'payoff' syndrome. This means that you are getting a real or imagined reward for staying in an unfulfilled world of limited thinking. For example:

- By not having a relationship do you feel you gain by avoiding the possibility of getting hurt?
- If you're not in perfect health, do you benefit by getting extra attention and affection or by avoiding too much work?
- If you find it hard to attract money, do you find that by being poor you resist the effort of living off your own wits and creativity?

A woman once came to see me who was very attached to living in a childlike fantasy world. She bemoaned the fact that opportunities never seemed to come her way, she never got the man, the job, the wealth. Yet whenever chances came for her to strike out in these areas she shrank back, cancelled engagements, became ill or simply messed it up. Her payoff was to remain in the seclusion of her ivory tower and never have to grow up or confront the vagaries of finite reality. At least this way she thought she wouldn't be disappointed. I pointed out that ultimately this was causing her tremendous pain and that everyone else was a child at heart too, doing their best to overcome their fears and achieve their dreams. Eventually she got the picture and she emerged from her safe but stifling ivory tower and into a fulfilled relationship and rewarding career.

It is very important to be completely honest with yourself about your motives for wanting and *not* wanting your desires. Remember that all your payoffs are actually time-wasting devices and avoidances of your greatness. Only by using your constant awareness and discipline to reject them and stay focused on your positive motives can you build up enough true power to fulfil your desires.

Surrender

When you have made all the right moves towards achieving your goal there is one last step for you to take. You must surrender your attachment to achieving it and discover the middle way between staying totally focused on it and being able to hand over to a higher power your chance of getting it. This is because if you form undue, fearful attachments to finite things you will always be ultimately disappointed. If you convince yourself that there is something in this world that you will die without, you're right! You will die *without it* just as you were born *without it*. You came into the world with nothing material and you will leave with nothing material. Making your happiness depend on the constantly shifting sands of finite reality can never make you feel truly safe.

If, for example, your dream is to make masses of money and you believe that without this you cannot be happy and at peace, it is the duty of the universal intelligence to show you your mistaken thinking. Instead of being given your dream millions, you might at first find yourself with much less. Otherwise as soon as your wealth arrived you would be forever worrying about how to hold on to it. This would prevent you from enjoying it and experiencing your natural birthright of peace.

And have you ever wanted a relationship so much that it hurt? Have you felt that if you could not be with the person of your desires then you couldn't be happy? As you thought about them day and night you would spin right out of your centeredness. If you finally managed to begin a relationship with them, you probably spent all your time worrying that you might lose them, because you had actually lost sight of the attractiveness of your own authentic power.

Generally, you will not be given something that is going to disempower you, (unless disempowerment is part of an essential lesson you need to learn). First you must prove that you can handle the achievement of your dreams in a responsible fashion. Once you can approach your goals from the perspective of your infinite self, you will become a healthy magnet for them. The only way that you can truly enjoy material things is to accept that they are all on loan from the earthly reality that you are currently passing through. One day you will come to realize that you are simply an eternal essence in need of nothing except love. In the meantime, go after your dreams with joy and vigour and when you find them, accept them graciously as fleeting gifts from a permanent source of abundance.

Thinking Big, Starting Small

The longest journey, as they say, begins with a single step. In every moment we are creating our own reality and we can either make it one of progress or stultification. We have all experienced times of being 'on a roll' where everything just seems to flow. These are the times when nothing seems an effort and every action flows easily into the next as we gather momentum. The only problem is that we can't always remember how we got into this groove in the first place!

You can learn to kick-start this process by taking some very simple steps. To get some kind of motivation going in your life, start with the small stuff. It's amazing how much we are affected by the minutiae of our lives and how taking control of them can become a starting point for major life changes. The places where you spend a lot of time are energetically very powerful for you. If there is a light bulb that needs changing in your home or a picture that needs straightening or a drawer that needs tidying, every time you come into contact with such things and do nothing about them, they will subliminally give you the message that you are ineffectual. This will make you feel bad and before you know it you'll find yourself feeling disgruntled and frustrated without understanding why.

So, start by carrying out the small jobs. Empty your overflowing bins, make those long overdue calls or sort out your paperwork. You will feel an instant surge of accomplishment after completing each task and you can then use this to propel you onto the next action. As you take these small steps, you will gather momentum and with it the desire to keep going. You'll soon be in full flow. All you need is a little discipline in the first place.

The ultimate responsibility for your life rests with you. If you want to stay in a rut you will. But if you are truly ready to expand and grow into the beauty, power and wisdom of Spiritual Fitness, you can begin right now. In a moment we will come to the exercises of the first Inner WorkOut that can transport you into a new, authentic and fulfilling reality. Before that, here is a brief review of the principles of motivation recharge.

REVIEW

The basic obstacles to getting yourself motivated are fear of the unknown and fear of failure. These are convenient distractions to mask your true fear which is the fear of your own greatness.

Putting off living your soul's true purpose can only make you unhappy, because your true happiness depends on your living honestly at a soul level.

There is a simple formula you can use to get yourself to take action: what, why, how.

Check out any payoffs you have been getting for staying stuck in your old, ineffectual patterns. Consciously eliminate them and focus on your soul's desires and journey.

When you have a clear sense of who you truly are and what it is you really want, make a concerted effort to achieve your soul's dream and then surrender the process up to your higher power.

Begin this life-changing process with manageable steps that you can take immediately in your everyday life.

THE INNER WORKOUT

The exercises that follow at the end of every WorkOut offer practical techniques for you to apply in your everyday life. Some can be done immediately and others are best extended over a period of seven days. Each is designed to give you quick and powerful results in your life.

All of the exercises in this course have a 'domino' effect. As you work consistently on one area and achieve success in it, you'll be able to apply the same principles to other areas to achieve similar success.

Of course, if you don't perform any of these exercises you won't get their benefits! So before we start you might like to consider that the process here is as important as the content. This means that your reaction to doing these exercises is precisely mirroring your attitude to the rest of your life. It will tell you as much about yourself as actually doing the exercises themselves.

For example, here are some of the reactions that you may find yourself experiencing that will reflect to you your current state of being. They are followed by *reflections* on what these reactions reveal about you.

'I hate doing this kind of thing; it's such an effort. I'd much rather just read the book and see what I think about it all at the end.'
You feel safe standing on the sidelines, without having a full hands-on experience of life. You form judgments from your rational experience and avoid any discomfort that too much involvement and inner searching might create.

'I can't do these now because I haven't got the time.'
Do you often find yourself feeling pressurized, stressed and powerless?

'I haven't got a pen and paper to hand. I think I'll do it tomorrow.'
Are you the type who complains that nothing seems to happen in your life?

'I have to do these before I can go on to read any more. I do hope I can understand everything and get it all right'.
Rules are rules and there is a set order to everything in the universe. At least you hope that's how it is, or your whole world may crumble!

'Okay, here's a chance for me to get involved and really see if and how this works.'
Your enthusiasm is balanced with practicality and curiosity. You are prepared to unearth some of life's secrets come what may.

'This book is so fantastic and I'm enjoying it so much, I'm going to read as much as I can and then come back to these exercises before I put the book down.'
You remind me of myself! Today is important but not half as much as tomorrow. You want the whole picture but you'd like it yesterday. If you really do come back and complete these exercises, congratulations! You are learning to temper your natural exuberance with a more steady approach to the practicalities of life.

So, if you're now ready to exercise your spiritual muscles, let's begin.

1   You can use this exercise to get yourself focused before you undertake any task, from making a phone call to attending a meeting, spending time with a loved one or simply going shopping. It will give you automatic centeredness and save you time and energy.

In a moment, close your eyes, take a few deep breaths, turn your awareness inside yourself and ask your heart the following three simple questions. For each question take only the first *one word* answer that comes to you. (Unlike your logical, rational mind, your intuition does not need to explain itself. An instant one-word answer is all you need). If you feel you can't find a word then just guess. Say to yourself, 'If I knew it would probably be ...' Whatever comes to you will be coming from your subconscious mind which is all that matters.

Okay, close your eyes, breathe deeply, focus inside for a moment and then gently open your eyes ...

Ask yourself this question: 'What do I want to achieve from following this course?' Quickly close your eyes and allow the first word that comes to you to present itself. When you have done this gently open your eyes again ...

Now ask yourself: 'How do I need to be to achieve that?' Again quickly close your eyes and take the first word that comes to you, then open your eyes ...

Finally ask yourself: 'How am I feeling now?' Again close your eyes and wait for the next word to come, and then allow your eyes to open ...

At this point, you may well find that there is a discrepancy between how you are feeling now and how you need to feel to achieve the result that you want. In other words, there is a discrepancy between your second and third answers. For example, you may need to be 'focused' but currently find yourself feeling restless. Next, close your eyes and go inside one last time. For the next few moments, affirm over and over to yourself your second answer, the one word that tells you how you need to be to get the result that you want. Either silently or out loud repeat it to yourself, as in the phrase, 'I am' or 'I have' this quality, or visualize yourself acting out this quality or feel it flooding throughout your whole being. You can do this now for a few moments ...

You have now aligned your subconscious and conscious minds to act in a way that is congruent with your deepest truth. This will make you much more powerful and effective in all your dealings.

2 Write down one thing that you would really like to manifest in your life. Think big and positively and be as clear as you can about what this one thing is.

Next, write down all your reasons for wanting to have it.

Then write down all the payoffs you get by not having it.

Now take a moment to think about the consequences of each of these. Do you really want to stay stuck? Close your eyes and imagine you are at the end of your life. As you look back, notice how you would feel if you continued avoiding your natural greatness for the rest of your lifetime. Make this projection as real as you can ...

Next close your eyes and imagine again that you are at the end of your life and this time notice how good you would feel if you had taken that leap and how your life would look when you had. Make this projection as real as you can ...

So now you should have a preferred outcome and I would hope and imagine that this involves you taking a leap of faith and going for your dream. If this is so, then I would also imagine that by now you are pretty certain that this is the course of action you want to take. However, just to be on the safe side, as soon as you can talk to someone about your plans with enough conviction that you are able to convince them you are serious. As you convince another you will also convince yourself.

Now write down five concrete steps that you can take in the next week to achieve your goals. It doesn't matter how small they are – they may be simple things like tidying your house or making a long-postponed phone call. At this stage you don't need to hand in your notice or put your house up for sale unless you are feeling very courageous and centred!

When you have written down these steps, also take these to the person you had to convince about your desire for your goal and tell them about your proposed tasks. Then promise to come back in a week's time with an update on your progress. It's so much easier for us to get motivated when we know that there is someone to whom we have to answer other than ourselves.

3 Look around your home and workplace. What little niggling jobs have you been putting off for days, weeks or even months. To get yourself going, DO AT LEAST ONE OF THEM RIGHT NOW!

SOUL DETOX

'The egg must break before the bird can fly'

Tennyson

If you have followed the exercises in WorkOut One you should now have some idea of what it is you want out of life. You may have recognized your payoffs for not going after it until now and you may have already begun to move away from them. The next question you need to ask yourself is 'Am I *ready* to receive what I want? Is there a clear space in my life for it and am I the person I need to be to accommodate and appreciate this exciting, new lifestyle?' This week we'll look at the next step on your path to Spiritual Fitness. This involves preparation through purification. This is perhaps the most challenging of all the WorkOuts because it deals with core issues that you may have chosen to ignore for much of your life. Take it as slowly as you need and understand that, just as in life, when you get beyond this something easier is around the corner!

THE THREE BASIC TOOLS OF SOUL DETOX

1 Understand Your Sensitivity

Before you can *get* the best out of yourself you have to know what *brings out* the best in you. You need to understand your sensitivity, be totally honest with yourself about your life and then have the courage to change what isn't working. It is only when you are clear of anything or anyone that doesn't reflect who you truly are at your highest level that you are at your most effective and powerful. When you are *clear* and surrounded by the optimum conditions for your true nature then you can expect to receive the most positive responses from the world around you. So, let's take a look at what it means to be clear.

Every thing in this universe, animate or inanimate, has an energy of its own. Some energies will be compatible with yours and some won't. Some people and places will leave you feeling drained, confused or irritated and others will make you feel uplifted, focused and balanced. It is very important that wherever possible you stay clear of energies that affect you negatively.

Most of us have far more heightened levels of subconscious aware-ness and sensitivity than we appreciate. For example, have you ever felt absolutely great one minute and then the next moment, for no appar-ent reason, felt absolutely … not great? This is because you are an elaborate energy radar. Every moment you are picking up signals from the energies around you, most of which are fear-based. Sometimes these are subtle, as in a person's crestfallen body language or the tone of embittered resignation in someone's voice, and sometimes they are really obvious – as a child, you may have heard a negative mantra of 'No, you'd better not do that' or 'We can't afford it' and so on.

We are rarely taught to be aware of our extreme sensitivity and therefore we follow earth level explanations for the changes this sensi-tivity can produce. So, for instance, you may assume that you are being irrationally moody, a victim of the latest emotional virus syndrome or even a clinical depressive. Nobody ever tells you that you may be a well-adjusted but sensitive soul who is attempting to align yourself with an unbalanced environment. The time has now come for you to look at exactly whose earth level rules you have been following.

Your sensitivity is your best guide in helping you to detox your soul. If you want to feel good, then start by spending time around the people and places that make you feel good and avoiding the ones that don't. If you feel that for the moment you're stuck with your co-workers/ family/place of abode, you can start by changing your *inner* world, by changing the way you *feel* about your outer world. This is where you have absolute control, as we shall see later in this WorkOut. The most important thing for you to know is that people treat you the way that you allow them to. As you develop your feelings of self-worth, your very purity and strength will begin to purge out anything and anyone negative surrounding you. You will also start to attract people and situations that honour who you truly are and enhance your own positive energy. Eventually, this will lead to changes in your external environment.

So, your detox begins with an awareness of your sensitivity and true needs. You must ask yourself, 'Which environment, what kind of people, which climate, what foods, entertainment, physical exercises and spiritual practices are best suited to who I truly am?' Most importantly, also start asking yourself, 'Which of my thoughts and belief systems serve my highest good and which patterns of thinking are toxic to my entire system?' (We shall be examining these in depth in the following section, 'The Detox Process'). Often it's only when we start to eliminate these toxic states from our lives and distance ourselves from old modes of behaviour that we can begin to appreciate how much of a negative impact they had on our lives. For instance, you might:

■ look back at past destructive relationships and wonder why you stayed in them for so long.
■ go back to visit your former workplace and realize just how oppressive and limiting it was for you.

consider a food/drink/drug you once consumed on a regular basis and know that your cleansed system simply couldn't handle it now.

In learning to understand your sensitivity, you may at first find it difficult to know which of your thoughts, likes and dislikes are your own and which ones you have absorbed from your environment. Once you have ascertained which are your own preferences in each area of your life, you can start to say 'yes' and 'no' to the world around you, based on your knowledge of your authentic needs and tastes. This way you'll begin to build your spiritual power base.

2 Take an Honest Look at Yourself

Once you start to understand your sensitivity you must also be ready to face the truth that this process reveals. One of the major tenets of Spiritual Fitness is absolute truth and the more deeply you are prepared to examine your soul's level of alignment and balance, the more effective your way forward will be. As the saying goes, 'You must get real to heal.' In other words, your unhappiness equals the size of the lie you are living.

Anything that is out of sync with your natural rhythm or vibration will tip you off balance and cause you pain. Just as it is uncomfortable to wear something that doesn't fit you. Whatever image you choose to present to the world will be mirrored back to you. If you act tough, your experiences will be of a tough world. If you make out that you are weak, you will be treated accordingly. The world is actually a neutral place and it takes its cue from you. What you radiate out is what you will draw back to you.

To be detoxified and spiritually fit, you need to discover who you truly are, know your value and then live it. Instead of burying your head in the sand and avoiding the more painful areas of your life, ask yourself what these areas of pain might tell you about your life and how these apparent problems are trying to help you to grow and move forward. (In a moment we'll look further at how you can do this).

Many people are unhappy in their jobs or relationships simply because they identify with and act out a one-dimensional role instead of being their fully rounded true selves. Do you ever feel that you are just the boss, the employee, the wife, husband, mother or father? To be fulfilled, you must be all of who you are at your purest level in every situation, at work, in your relationships and in social interactions. Living your truth doesn't always mean having to change your environment but instead can mean getting your environment to honour and reflect your essential self. In my many years working at a nightclub, I would frequently conduct relationship counselling with the office girls over my typewriter by day and then at night expound my spiritual theories with the club members over a bottle of champagne. They always seemed to leave happy and told me they had never met anyone like me in a nightclub before! They would then often appear at the workshops I ran on my days off.

As you develop your Spiritual Fitness, you will gradually feel strong enough to be your total self wherever you are. Authentic power comes when *you* can first be at peace with the truth of who you are, wherever you are, and then learn to hold that power when dealing with others.

3 Making Change Your Friend

As with all other kinds of purification, in order to detox your soul there will be certain parts of your old lifestyle that you will have to let go. You must accept change as a vital part of your life. And you will have to make some decisions. Do you really want to change? How committed are you to the process of change and all it will entail? How seriously do you take your spiritual well-being? How prepared are you to face the discomfort of being in-between realities, while the old and stultifying is replaced by the new and stimulating?

To progress to Spiritual Fitness, you must make change your friend and not resist the inevitable crumbling of illusory structures. Change involves recognizing and getting rid of old patterns – habits, beliefs, fears and the like – that no longer serve you. There will probably be some discomfort as you start to accept that what you once valued and believed was vital to your very existence is a superfluous crutch forcing you to limp along instead of allowing you to run free.

Many of us read the books, do the courses and follow the practices and then wonder why our life seems to have turned upside down. We are shocked when the inevitable change we have invoked rocks our illusory world. Trapped in a vapid quest for easy answers and quick fix solutions, we make our initial journey along the path of spiritual awakening to discover more about ourselves *as we are*. We don't really want to change, we just want to feel better about our old way of doing things. We want to feel less pain about our relationship, job or finances *within our old structures*. We try to make absolute truth perpetuate the status quo of our world of absolute illusion.

For example, you may at first find yourself using your new understanding of co-dependent relationships to excuse rather than end your destructive partnership. Or you may rely on your developing faith to prolong your extreme, self-destructive smoking or drinking habits, happily chanting 'It's okay, the universe will tell me when to stop before it's too late'. (The universe is more than generous and indulgent of our faith, but it's not there to support our dysfunctional habits). And so we cover up the stagnant relationship, the dead end job, the tedious routine with glimpses of a new reality which, if taken seriously, would blow our redundant old habits out of the water. A little feng shui here, a few essential oils there and some crystals on the coffee table are not enough. You must be ready for deep, life-transforming change.

Genuine growth offers great rewards. As you wake up from your everyday (un)reality, you will really begin to experience life to the full. Suddenly your relationship makes more sense to you, (or if it doesn't, you won't mind changing it for a better one!). Your job will become more interesting as you view it as either an opportunity for growth or a means to support you while you get started on what it is you really came here to do. Your health and your appearance will improve as you radiate more and more honesty and vitality from the core of your being. Just as with physical exercise, the more you change and get spiritually fitter, the better you will feel and the more you will want to do it. Change itself becomes a familiar and safe place to be.

THE DETOX PROCESS

With your tools of sensitivity, honesty and openness to change, you can now get started on the detox process. Let's take a look at one of our earlier questions – 'Which thoughts and belief systems serve your highest good and which patterns of thinking are toxic to your entire system?'

Feng Shui for the Mind

In recent years feng shui and the art of space clearing have become mainstream global concepts. We have learned to pay attention to what goes where, what 'feels' right and how to keep our outer environment clutter free. Yet if you want to experience true positive change and alignment in your life you must also remember to do some space clearing on your inner environment and feng shui your mind. To do this you need to realize that you actually *choose* what happens within your mind. Therefore, you must be careful what thoughts you allow in and how you choose to store them. You have to keep noticing and acknowledging your true feelings and keep your mind clear of disempowering toxic patterns.

These patterns are very insidious and powerful because so much of our thinking is dictated by an accumulation of outside influences. It is said that we have approximately 60,000 thoughts each day, most of which are repeats of old thoughts and opinions – ours or someone else's. Since you are the only person to actually hear, see and feel the frenetic, relentless assault of your each and every thought, 365 days of the year, 24 hours a day, 60 minutes per hour and 60 seconds per minute, you are therefore spending most of your time in a self-induced trance of second-hand thinking. This also means that each *new* experience you have is being judged against beliefs that you have based on your *old* experiences. Wouldn't it be interesting if you just stopped for a moment and asked yourself in each situation, 'How much of this am I experiencing as if for the first time? How much of me is relating from my true self to this? And do I even know who my real true self is?'

You can start to detoxify your mind and thoughts by breaking out of your trance of automatic thinking. We are creatures of habit who spend most of our time on autopilot. Have you ever gone to dial a new phone number similar to that of a close friend, only to find that you dial the latter *without thinking*? Or have you taken a familiar route from your home *without thinking* instead of going to the destination you intended? Our habits have the effect of making our future a stale rehash of our past. With discipline and conscious effort, you can break your toxic thought patterns and address each new situation uncluttered by past opinions, likes and dislikes. To do this you can begin by asking yourself how many toxic opinions you hold as unassailable that are in fact no longer serving you. What are your beliefs about money, sex, love or happiness? And are you ready to accept that there are new ways of looking at these areas of your life?

Our beliefs are the most ingrained and powerful aspect of our minds. If your beliefs are small and limiting then neither your imagination, nor your willpower nor your creativity will be able to flow. So what exactly are beliefs? They are the way in which you choose to interpret or judge the reality of the world you perceive. Here's how your beliefs control all your life experiences. To have any experience, you first have to take an *action*. For example, to have the *experience* of reading this book, you first had to take the *action* of opening it. And where do your actions come from? They come from your *thoughts*. Before you could take the *action* of opening the book, you first had to have a *thought* that you wanted to do so. And where do your thoughts come from? They come from your *belief* systems.

This means that if, for example, you believed that this book would explode when you opened it, then you would leave it closed. You open it only because you believe that to do so may in some way be rewarding for you and this belief in turn gives you the *experience* of looking for that reward. So your *beliefs* control your *thoughts*, which create your *actions*, which form your *experiences*. And where do your beliefs come from? They come from the *interpretations* or *judgments* you make of your experiences. Around and around it all goes, in a seemingly never-ending loop.

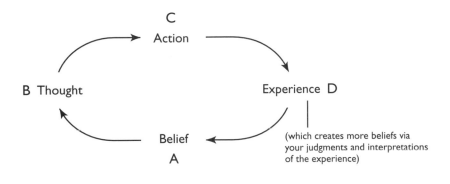

The Experience Equation

Dissolving Negative Beliefs

As with so much of your thinking, this loop will often be founded on negative beliefs. You can hear it in the voice that tells you 'You can't do that' or 'Things never work out the way you hope'. To break out from this loop, you must first acknowledge that your beliefs are your choice and that therefore you can change them. You can seize back your power by re-interpreting your life from a higher and more fulfilling perspective. *A Course In Miracles* tells us that when we are not at peace we are indulging in mistaken thinking in our interpretation of life. We are not understanding life at its highest level and are not seeing its gifts to us. Somewhere, at some point, you created these negative beliefs based on fear. Now you have the chance to find a more meaningful, soul level reason for the events that occur around you and as you do so, your beliefs about them will immediately change. Your more positive *interpretations* will create *new beliefs* and therefore *new experiences*.

For example, if you have a belief that relationships are painful based on your experience of past hurts, this belief will continue to cause you to experience painful relationships if you don't change it. However, if you move up to a soul level perspective, you'll see that you are carrying around issues and wounds that you still have not dealt with. You will realize that each partner you attract to you is on a soul level offering you the opportunity to confront the fear behind your pain and find the courage to overcome it. This new perspective can alter your beliefs about relationships and will eventually lead you to experience more healthy partnerships. (We shall look at the relationship issue more closely in WorkOut Four).

A woman came to me who was very creative but who did not believe in her natural talents. She complained that her life was dull and unrewarding, yet whenever opportunities were presented to her to make money and a career out of her abilities, she would back away from them. Her beliefs told her that she would never be good enough to succeed and, of course, since she didn't try she didn't succeed. Her beliefs had become a self-fulfilling prophecy. I pointed out to her that behind all this negativity was a fear of her own greatness. On a soul level, life was inviting her to express her full talented potential. Until she chose to believe in her creativity, she would continue to experience frustration and a general malaise. Eventually, she acknowledged this and, as she began to form more empowering beliefs for herself and with them more creative experiences, her life became much more fulfilling.

So then, the first way to dissolve your patterns of toxic thinking is to trace your beliefs back to the source and see how they are mistaken in

some way. Ask yourself when exactly you took on these negative beliefs and realize that there was once a time when you didn't have them.
We come into this world with no beliefs at all and only form them in
relation to the world we find around us. This world deals in the cur-
rency of fear and many of our early beliefs are tinged with the fear of
mistaken thinking. Try to remember how much better life felt before
you had these beliefs. You can also ask yourself how many of them are
now just a convenient way of distracting yourself from your greatness.

You may, for instance, be able to remember the first time that you
adopted limiting beliefs about money. Perhaps you heard your parents
say that 'Money doesn't grow on trees' or saw your family struggle
through hard times because they were poor. At this point you may
have formed beliefs about the power of money (or the lack of it) to
cause hardship. In turn this may have affected your relationship to
money, causing you to feel hard done by and believing that all financial gain involves struggle of some kind. As we have seen, this attitude
will then create life experiences to match your beliefs.

So, remember that there was a time when as a very small child you
had no opinions about money. If you can return to that blank state
inside yourself, you can form new beliefs that will support you and
help create a whole new reality. You can choose to adopt new beliefs
which say that 'The best things in life are free' or that the universe will
always reward you for using your talents. Immediately, these attitudes
will lighten your demeanour and make you more attractive to others.
They will want to help you and will be happy to give you a fair
exchange for your unique set of gifts. In this way you will come to
understand that your old beliefs about money were second-hand and
based on fear.

Finally, the most important thing to remember about your beliefs is
that they are a habit. To change your beliefs may be one of the most
difficult things you have to do because they provide you with the apparent safety of familiarity that we all crave. To change them needs
your constant vigilance, application, discipline and determination. The

best tool you have to help you in this task is your memory. Each time you are about to go down the same old road, moving from your beliefs to your thoughts, from there to your actions and then experiences, simply remember where this road took you last time (and all the times before that). Consistently and determinedly consider the consequences before you take action, then create new pathways in your mind that will lead you to a more positive outcome. Gradually you will find yourself at the start of a fresh and uplifting way forward.

The Detoxifying Power of Forgiveness

The second way to dissolve your negative beliefs is by taking the fast-track route of forgiveness. As an example, let's say that you have formed a strong negative opinion about the opposite sex following some unpleasant childhood experiences. The beliefs that you formed from your interpretation of these experiences have hindered your enjoyment of life until today. At this moment you have a choice. You can either be right, (and justifiably outraged at what you endured) or you can be at peace, by freeing yourself from further pain through forgiveness. I won't pretend that in some cases this second choice isn't an extremely difficult one to make and there are those who believe that they are unable to reach forgiveness and the peace that it offers. To these people I would recount this true story of the power of forgiveness.

During the Second World War, a man was forced to watch his wife and children being massacred by the Nazis before his eyes. Immediately he begged the soldiers to take his life too but they refused, saying they wanted him kept alive because he spoke several languages. At this point he realized he had only one choice available to him – either to hate his captors or to forgive them. He delved deep inside his heart and somehow managed to find forgiveness by recognizing the great fear, pain and terrible mistaken thinking that was behind their actions. When a few years later his concentration camp was liberated, the allied forces thanked him for being such a help to the other prisoners and judging him by his almost robust appearance, asked him how he had suddenly turned up at the camp. When he told them he had been there for years, they learned how the healing power of forgiveness and love can triumph over the most horrifying actions produced by fear and mistaken thinking.

To forgive means to let go of past judgments. As we have seen, all your beliefs are based on your interpretations or judgments of what you have experienced. If you think about it you will find that it is impossible to maintain a peaceful state of mind and at the same time have a judgmental thought about another. If you don't believe me, try it right now!

Breathe deeply a few times, let your mind wander and imagine you are in your favourite place on earth. Make it as real as you can, see the colours, hear the sounds and feel the textures all around you …

Feel a great sense of peace beginning to flood through you …

Now think of someone who really irritates you …

You will notice how your clear state of peace instantly becomes cloudy and agitated when you fill your mind with negative judgments. Soul level forgiveness is not about condoning or absolving someone's outrageous behaviour. It means escaping from the painful zone of dealing with them only on an earthly, fear-based and limiting level. To forgive truly you must lift up your thinking to a soul level. Somehow you can find a present-day gift in this memory. What have you learned from it? How has it contributed to the understanding and expansion of your soul? How can you share this lesson with others so that they can avoid similar pain? Look at the perpetrator of your pain and see what pain and fear of their own brought them to act that way. You forgive another not so much to set them free but to set yourself free. This brings about a healing closure. They will pursue their own journey with its own lessons at their own pace. You return to peace. Once again, peace is your choice.

Clearing Your Emotions

Once you have cleaned up your thought processes, you can take a look at your emotions. From time to time we all experience painful toxic emotions. They are what some psychologists refer to as our 'shadow' side and they include feelings such as fear, self-doubt, low self-esteem, bitterness, anger, guilt, jealousy and self-denial. Ever suffered from any of these? Welcome to the human race! Since our healthiest thinking comes from avoiding being judgmental, first learn not to worry that your shadow feelings are bad or wrong, but instead accept them as a part of your human experience in this earthly world. You will want to reduce your experience of them as much as possible but to detox your emotions doesn't mean never feeling upset in any way ever again. It means sometimes having to experience these emotions while simultaneously, on a soul level, being able to see them as invitations for growth. This automatically softens their negative impact.

If, for instance, you find yourself jealous of someone at work, it's very likely that beneath this emotion you are hiding feelings of inadequacy. Instead of resenting their success, first be truthful with yourself and admit that underneath it all you imagine, for whatever reason, that you are incapable of being as successful yourself. Then raise yourself up to a soul level and see the invitation this emotion offers you to dig deep inside yourself and have the courage to shine and succeed in your own way. (Here again you will notice the increasingly familiar truth that your greatest fear is the fear of your own greatness).

As with your beliefs, many of your emotions have evolved from your experiences of the world around you. Despite your apparent array of emotions, there are ultimately only two at the basis of all others and these are fear and love. Your natural state is one of love. If you don't believe me, then take a look at the next baby you encounter. Babies, that is human beings who are fresh from the source, are filled to overflowing with natural love, and this is the original basic state of all of us. To start to detox your emotions, you'll need to strip back to this natural, open and loving state that may by now be buried deep inside you.

Again as with your beliefs, your emotions become ingrained and you identify with them as your own and as who you are. So you believe you are 'happy' or 'sad', 'excited' or 'depressed' and you come to regard your emotions as your whole self. The first thing to remember is that many of your emotions do not even originate with you – you are picking them up from the people around you. If you have ever felt down after visiting a grieving friend or on a high after sharing in another's triumph, you will recognize this syndrome.

I once saw an advert for AIDS awareness which suggested that every time you have sex with someone, then, in health terms, you may as well also be sleeping with every one of their previous partners. For me this was an accurate metaphor for the energy transfers that take place whenever we have *any* sort of contact with another person. You are the sum of all your experiences. Every single encounter leaves an imprint on your soul. This is why, under regression or in times of trauma, people suddenly find themselves reliving experiences they previously could not recall. Every minute of every day, with your every interaction, whether buying a bus ticket, shopping, listening to the praise or criticism of others or providing a shoulder for their woes, you pick up the energy of those around you. Your emotional state, your personality and even your physical body are all composites of every thought, word and human interaction you have ever experienced. This is why it is so important to learn to understand your own feelings and be able to recognize which ones are your own and which ones you are picking up from others.

Have you ever noticed how you feel sluggish around some people but totally relaxed and yet fully alive around others? Have you ever had the experience of feeling so exhausted when you are at a party that you simply must go home, only to find when you get there that you are now wide awake? This is because your energy was being drained by the energy of those around you since it was not congruent with your own. Your companions' emotions were different from yours but in their company you were starting to take on their emotions as your own. This meant that you were suppressing your true feelings. Whenever we are forced into a situation where we cannot express ourselves honestly we suffer from what I call non-alignment fatigue. It occurs whenever you can't express your natural exuberance, quietness, optimism or sadness in any situation.

THE POWER OF INTUITION

Taking on unsympathetic energies can make you confused and not fully open to the world around you. At these times your mind and your emotions get polluted and you lose your centre of reality – what you really know to be true about yourself. You suddenly feel stressed, exhausted, overwhelmed or upset. Worse still, you assume that all of this psychic debris is yours! The best tool you have to clear yourself is your intuition. Your intuition goes straight to the heart of feelings and thoughts. By definition it doesn't need any rational explanation. It speaks to you the moment you enter a room and have that 'gut' feeling of not belonging there. Instead of reaching for a drink or engaging in forced conversation, act on your true feelings and turn round and leave. Your intuition also manifests when you pick up the phone and your heart sinks as you hear a familiar voice that always drains you. Before you find your energy beginning to slump, learn to make your excuses and end the call.

Traditionally, we have been taught to suppress our intuition. Those who act on their hunches are thought to be slightly reckless, (although they are fêted if those hunches prove to be consistently correct). Those who pay too much attention to their 'heart' and only do things that 'feel right', rejecting all else without logical explanation, may be considered neurotic or flaky. And so you need to develop a working relationship with your intuition and develop a respect for it. Like any other faculty you possess, it will become stronger the more that you use it.

THE HEALING POWER OF SELF-LOVE

Again, as with detoxing your beliefs, the other main tool for clearing your negative emotions is forgiveness and the most important person to forgive is yourself. We all find it difficult to like ourselves when we are having negative feelings unless we are being particularly self-righteous. So go easy on yourself and realize that by learning to love yourself unconditionally, you can start to soften your toxic emotions. There is much talk within modern spiritual movements of the need for us to love ourselves. For years I found this a very confusing concept as I tried to follow suggested formulas. For instance, whenever I took myself out on a dinner date, I would end up eating and drinking enough for two and feeling quite toxic by the end of it all! Similarly, when making grand gestures of buying myself flowers or treating myself to expensive gifts I couldn't convince myself that the process wasn't contrived.

It was only when I became quite ill that I began to realize what loving myself truly meant. Firstly, it meant protecting and nurturing myself and keeping anything that was harmful away from me. I was forced to recognize what weakens my body and soul and had to learn to avoid all the things and people that did. Self-love is, of course, equated with self-worth. It means honouring what works for you and rejecting what is not acceptable to you. Self-love is also doing what makes you happy and finding out what brings you joy and peace, and then incorporating that into your life. For instance, remember what makes you laugh and make sure it features strongly in your life.

In learning to nurture yourself, you can begin to build your self-love and inner strength by starting with the small things. For example, in the past I would sometimes find myself eating food at home that was a little past its sell-by date. If vegetables looked a bit rotten here or there, then I'd simply cut off the offending piece and make do with the remainder. Then one day I found myself wondering if I would present this kind of food to someone I really loved and I came up with the answer 'no'. After this I started to feed myself only the best food that

I had available to me. This process, though simple in itself, gave me a subtle but strong message that I was also worthy of the love I found it so easy to give to others.

Onto this awareness I built other conditions that made me treat myself with more consideration. I started to go to bed when I was tired instead of staying up and fighting to stay awake to get things done. I didn't answer the phone if I felt I needed peace. Slowly but surely I created a respect for myself and began to get a sense of what was tolerable for me and what wasn't. Gradually I experienced this spilling over into the rest of my life and into my dealings with others. I found that I was more able to stand up for myself, refuse anything that didn't feel right for me and meet my true needs. Through this I also started to clear many of my negative emotions. I had much less need for anger, panic or resentment because I was able to express my true needs and feelings directly before they could distort into secondary negative emotions. I discovered that there is a lot more to loving yourself than taking yourself out on dates. It means learning to *cherish* yourself and revere who you are as a divine being passing through an earthly incarnation.

PURIFYING YOUR SURROUNDINGS

Once you have cleared your inner environment you also need to look at detoxing everything in your outer environment. It is amazing how much we are affected by influences from the material world. It is not just the obvious effects of busy traffic, tight schedules, ringing phones, background TV and overcrowded shops that stress us. It is also the more subtle influences of the books we read, the music we listen to, the movies we watch and even the food that we eat. The most strengthening antidote to all of this is of meditation. This enables you to find a centre of calm amidst this hectic world by working from the inside out. We shall come to this in WorkOut Five, but for now let's look at what can be done about purifying your environment from the outside in.

The Healing Power of Silence

As you grow more aware of your own sensitivity and start to follow your intuition and acknowledge your true feelings, you will find it easy to assess the effects that your outer world has on you. At times you will find the need to withdraw and re-align yourself with your own centre. You'll find that silence and solitude become two essential ingredients for your detox from your environment. Discovering the healing power of silence has been one of the great awakenings on my quest for Spiritual Fitness, since for many years I was afraid to be left alone with the sound of my own inner voice. From my teens I have been a great collector of records and CDs. In days gone by, I would do almost everything with some kind of music playing in the background. What I had failed to notice was that each note in a minor key, a sad lyric or the poignant memory that it evoked had a subliminally weakening effect on me. I could wake up happy, turn on the radio or play a CD and then, without knowing why, find my spirits dropping for no apparent reason. Even up-tempo happy songs could jar on me if I was feeling in an especially tranquil, mellow sort of mood. As I began to spend more of my time without this obligatory musical 'soundtrack', I noticed that I felt more in control of my emotions.

Now, when I lead retreats to my spiritual home in Sedona, Arizona we spend much of our time meditating in the mountains in solitude and silence. Through the stillness that this creates within us, healing, revelation and transformation are able to take place. Silence and solitude awaken in us a sense of space that connects us to the infinite life force that flows through us. Since you can only experience this vital and powerful purification when you are quiet and alone, you must be sure to give yourself at least a few minutes of both of these states each day.

If you do not have a room that you can set aside in your home as a place of peace, then at least you can build yourself an altar to whatever force you hold sacred and sit before it each day to return you to your inner centred self-awareness. Anywhere will do, as long as you regard it with a sense of reverence. I once heard of a woman who lived in such a small space that she had to retreat underneath her kitchen table as her designated place of reverence and solitude!

The Healing Power of Spontaneity

The next thing that you can do to detox your external environment is to release yourself from the rigid routine that attaches you to it. It is amazing how much we come to rely on our outer habits to give us a sense of who we are. For example, do you have to have your home arranged in a set way, as in 'The remote control *always* stays on this chair!'? Do you have a certain outfit that you must wear to feel good, as in 'Where's my favourite shirt?' Do you have fixed tasks that only you must do at work, as in 'That's *my* job and nobody does it as well as me!'?

Your most powerful habitual behaviour is usually at its most evident in your first waking moments. For a few blissful milliseconds, fresh from the hinterland of sleep, your soul feels free and lies peacefully adjusting to consciousness. Then suddenly you remember who it is you are supposed to be! Before you know it, you have downloaded the programme of your personal identity – your name, role, function, likes and dislikes. You grasp at this mantle of familiarity, suck in your aura and prepare to walk robot-like through the rest of your day, enslaved to your limiting self-image. Even before leaving your home, you invoke a restrictive routine that declares you must wash, eat and dress in a certain order or you will feel all day as if you had literally got out of the wrong side of bed. This is why houseguests can be such a challenge to us – an occupied bathroom or an empty coffee jar can shake our early morning identity to the core. These 'intruders' violate the rituals by which we define our control over life. In fact, if you want to fast-track to enlightenment, invite someone very unlike you to stay for a month!

These habitual responses to your environment keep you stuck and hinder your spiritual growth. To experience the true power of Spiritual Fitness you must free yourself from anything that prevents you from being spontaneous in the moment. The true freedom of Spiritual Fitness comes from letting go of pre-ordained behaviour and creating a vibrant reality afresh each day.

Finding the Environment for Growth

The qualities of our physical surroundings, both at home and outside, influence our feelings tremendously. As we all know, we are each affected by the different types of weather around us and we have learned that for many people Seasonal Affective Disorder (SAD) plays a major part in the balance of the psyche. Yet it isn't just cloudy skies and short daylight hours that can affect us. For some people, too many continuous days of intense heat can be energy sapping. High winds can prove invigorating to some and enervating for others. While we can't yet control our climate to any significant degree, it's very helpful for you to become aware of your responses to it and so gear your life accordingly. Similarly, you can start to pay attention to the seasons and the cycles of the moon. For our ancestors this was an accepted way of life and many native peoples still allow themselves to be guided by the cycles of nature, instead of trying to conquer them. What we need to remember is that no matter how sophisticated we believe that we have become, we are still products of this earth and as such do much better when we live in alignment with her.

Landscapes, too, have a deep impact on the soul. They can serve to expand or constrict you as your inner landscape adapts to reflect the outer terrain. Cities tend to make you tighten up and open landscapes usually make you more loose and relaxed. If your current lifestyle does not allow you to spend as much time as you would like in your preferred landscape, (for example, beaches, mountains, deserts and lakes), then recreate as much of the desired ambience as you can in your own home. Since I first discovered the awesome majesty of the red rock mountains of Sedona, I have used photographs, furnishings and various adornments from there in my city home to trigger within me an instant memory of this sacred place.

The actual layout of your home can also have a profound effect on you. I have only a rudimentary knowledge of the art of feng shui but I do know that chaos in your outer environment will only serve to agitate and disrupt your inner world. It sends signals to you that you are out of control and overwhelmed. While there are many good books available on feng shui and space clearing, I believe that your best guide is your own intuition. As your sensitivity heightens, you will start to notice what makes you feel more or less at ease and you will be able to arrange your home accordingly. To begin this process, you can experiment with new positions of furniture and adornments and observe the different energies they create.

Time is also an important influence to consider. Some of us are night people and some are early morning types. Wherever possible, start to gear your life around the times of day that are most conducive for you. It's always best to work when you are wide-awake and rest when you are at a low ebb. When I write I find that I enjoy the uninterrupted peace of the night hours. Many writers I know tend to rise at 5 or 6am to begin their composing which is often the time that I am just going to bed. As with everything else in your external environment, your use of time will be most powerful for you if you align it with your own inner clock.

Sex and Soul Detox

I have heard it said that every time we have sex, the energy of our sexual partner stays with us for six weeks. Therefore, if you are having sex with more than one person in the next six weeks this probably means that your energy field will be getting pretty crowded! As with all your other interactions with others, you need to be sure that the sex you are having is the result of your authentic needs and desires and that it is serving your highest good. As most of us know through experience, sex can very easily open the door to the madness of our deepest insecurities. Here again, it is very important that you acknowledge your sensitivity and bring a soul level thinking approach to your sex life.

Soul level sex is the kind that will expand your spiritual awareness and allow your inner self to grow and blossom. It will make you open up in ways you may never have thought possible and connect you with a very deep level of self-awareness and oneness. It can help you to feel simultaneously the many different dimensions of reality that surround you and experience a sense of transcendence.

As we saw in the previous WorkOut, passion is one of our greatest motivators in blasting us out of our stale, frightened attachment to the earth level confines of familiarity. Yet precisely because of its enormous power, you must always be vigilant that the sexual energy you create with your partner nourishes rather than consumes you. It is very important that you feel safe and loved when you are engaging in any kind of intimacy and the Spiritual Fitness qualities of kindness, truth and trust must be present to ensure that your soul can be nurtured and advanced through sex. (We shall look at the relationship dynamics of sex in WorkOut Four).

Over the centuries, many spiritual traditions have advocated celibacy as a necessity on the path to spiritual awareness. Others such as tantra and some of the ancient pagan and goddess religions have viewed the tremendous energy generated by sex as part of a sacred ritual. For me, the same principles of soul detox apply here as elsewhere in your life. If you experiment with a period of energy cleansing either by abstention or by using heightened awareness in your sex life, you will soon discover your soul's true needs and how these can best be met through sex. Once again, your outer environment will align itself to your inner environment and you will be able to experience the joy and harmony this produces.

Detoxing with Food, Drink and Exercise

There are countless physical exercise and dietary regimes on offer to us and it is likely that somewhere amongst them is the right one for you. Using the tools that you are already developing, your sensitivity and your intuition will guide you to whichever one works best for you. For myself, I have found that drinking eight to ten glasses of water a day and eating unprocessed (preferably organic) foods, taking gentle exercise and generally avoiding stimulants such as caffeine and alcohol has helped me to raise my level of Spiritual Fitness. I have also found that there are other times when, as the old saying goes, 'A little of what you fancy does you good!' Perhaps the best advice I can give is to echo the words of one of my great teachers and recommend 'moderation in all things, including moderation!' There are lots of 'dos' and 'don'ts' suggested in this area so just remember to sprinkle plenty of fun and enjoyment in all that you do. When you find what works for you, make it most effective by sticking to it. Most important is that you are realistic in your expectations. If you really aren't the athletic kind then it is pointless making wild promises that you will jog three miles every day. You are setting yourself up for disappointment and frustration and thereby doing yourself more harm than good.

REVIEW

You are an extremely sensitive mechanism, constantly interacting with the world around you both on earth and soul levels. To get the most from your inner and outer environments you need to experience your life from the authentic truth of your soul level perspective.

Your negative, earth level interpretations of past experiences give rise to negative beliefs and, in turn, negative thoughts. You have the power to break out of this loop and create new experiences by reinterpreting past experiences from a soul level.

Your emotions are transitory and are not your whole self. In fact you often pick up negative feelings from those around you. The detoxifying power of self-love and forgiveness will heal you and set you free.

Set aside a period of silence and solitude in your every day life to balance and purify you.

Adapt your outer environment to bring out your natural inner joy and peace. In all things let your intuition guide you to all that works best for you.

THE INNER WORKOUT

1   Write down a paragraph about your morning routine and the way you like to get things done. For instance:

   ■ Do you *have* to shower or bath before eating?
   ■ Do you *always* listen to the same radio station?
   ■ Does your breakfast consist of the same food *every* day?

Now look over what you've written and try changing at least two actions for the next week. Notice how you start to feel different during the day after beginning from a place of greater fluidity. You may well find yourself feeling more free, creative and empowered.

2   Rate yourself out of ten in the following areas of your life:

   ■ your career
   ■ spirituality
   ■ health
   ■ relationship
   ■ creativity
   ■ finances.

Now write down a brief sentence on what would have to happen for you to have a number ten experience in each of these areas.

Next, briefly write down your limiting beliefs in each category that prevent you from getting there.

Finally, using a different piece of paper, write one sentence that is opposite to each of these limiting beliefs. For example, instead of 'money is the root of evil', you could say 'wealth creates generosity and gives me a way to help others'. Place this somewhere that you can read it each day for a week when you are relaxed and silent. You will be amazed at how quickly these new beliefs can start to create a new experience of reality for you, if you simply focus on them daily within your heart.

3   Impose a 'noise and company curfew' for at least fifteen minutes each day. It is vital that you create a space in your home to which you feel you can retreat and restore your sense of self. During this time you must have silence and solitude. This means no phone calls, answered door bells or any other interruptions. Other people will only take this as seriously as they see you taking it, so be prepared to impose your 'curfew' with firmness.

4   Get to know the sound of your own intuitive voice. If you don't know what your inner guide sounds like, how can you be expected to trust it? An easy way to develop this awareness is to ask yourself some 'yes' and 'no' questions to which you already know the answers. Try replying to each first with a resounding 'yes' and then replying to the same question with a 'no' and notice the difference inside. Does a true answer seem to come from a different part of your body than a false answer? Do they seem to have a different 'voice'? Does a false answer cause you any unease or physical discomfort?

Try this now by answering out loud only 'yes' to all the following questions, *even though you know that some of your 'yes' answers will be lies.* Sit or stand up straight, focus on your inner self and shout out a big 'yes' to every question.

- Are you a human being?
- Are you a fish?
- Are you sitting down?
- Are you standing up?
- Are you sitting on the ceiling?
- Are you a man?
- Are you a woman?
- Are you a bird?
- Are you alive?

So, did you notice a difference? Now repeat the above, this time answering with a loud 'no' to every question. Keep practising this exercise until you can be very clear on what your truth sounds and feels like.

When you have done this, apply this skill to your everyday life. As usual, start small and work your way up. What are your plans for the rest of the day? Think of one thing you feel you have to do. For example, do you feel you should go to the gym after an exhausting day at work?

Now ask yourself if this is really the right thing for you to do for your highest good today. Flash the question, 'Do I really want to go to the gym tonight?' into your mind and then allow the answer to flash up inside you and immediately take the first 'yes' or 'no' that comes to you. (Remember, your intuition is swift and needs no mental consideration).

Notice how that answer feels. Does it feel like the truth or a lie? If you want to double-check, try telling yourself the opposite and see how that feels. For example, your first answer was 'no', you don't want to go to the gym. Ask yourself the same question again and this time tell yourself 'yes'. Does that feel like the truth or a lie? You will soon feel confident enough to trust your first answers without the need to double-check.

Finally act on the information you have been given by your intuition. Keep using this technique until you naturally learn to follow the promptings of the higher power that is guiding you. At the end of each day, look back and see what you learned and how you benefited by following your own inner guidance.

MINDING YOUR LANGUAGE

**'You know, she speaks eighteen languages,
and she can't say "No" in any of them.'**

Dorothy Parker

If you've done all the exercises so far, you may well find your general awareness of life beginning to heighten. You may be starting to respond differently to situations, more calmly and with greater understanding. This week we now begin to gather pace. There is nothing different for you to do on a conscious level – just read on as usual. Simply know that on a subliminal level you are beginning to learn more quickly, as you open yourself up to new levels of understanding.

So far we have looked at how you can pull back from the world a little, clear up your life and get a sense of direction. Now we are ready to look at how you move outwardly towards the world around you through your language. As we shall see, there is a lot more to language than mere words. Here we will explore how you can begin to communicate from your real self and use the energy of words and the spaces in between them, as much as their direct meaning, to make yourself truly understood.

WHAT ARE WORDS?

First, let's look at exactly what words are. Words are the sounds and symbols you use to capture and convey your thoughts and feelings. This makes them extremely powerful. Through the words you use, you reach out to others and partly fulfil your innate need for connection. We all connect with each other primarily through language and touch. Since we touch far less than we speak, language is paramount in the way that we communicate. If you talk to those who are housebound and live alone, they will usually describe company and conversation as the things they miss most about the outside world. I can remember the times I used to visit a dear friend with muscular dystrophy. While others took her provisions and did her housework, she would always ask me just to sit and talk with her because it was this spoken connection that she missed most.

Language also helps to fulfil your need to give meaning to your world, by enabling you to define it. Once you can describe your reality, you can interpret your experiences and share them with others. Language is a vital tool in our everyday existence and so great is our need for it that we have even created sign language to represent words for those who cannot hear or speak. When we write words they are a pictorial representation of our thoughts and feelings. When we speak them, they are simply the cultivated noises we have created to communicate our inner voice to others.

Despite our apparent sophistication, the only way we differ in our speech from our earliest ancestors is that we now have some fancy grammar and a few hundred thousand more varieties of language systems at our disposal. Ultimately, our basic communication has not changed. Every time we open our mouths to speak to someone, we are actually saying 'This is who I am and this is what I think or want.' The 'ugh', 'ah' and wild gesticulating of cave man and woman has simply developed into such expressions as 'Would you please pass the salt?', 'I love you' or 'Go away!'. No matter how evolved we may think we have become, our language is still just a tool for us to get our point across.

How Words Work

As with your thoughts, you are the only one to see and hear *every* word you write and speak. Consequently your language has a very powerful affect on you. This is especially so because the words you use to describe your experiences help you to form your opinions about them. They help you to give them meaning and bring them into your conscious reality. For example, when you find yourself stretching and yawning, you'll suddenly tell yourself, 'I'm tired'. You will then consciously behave in a way that explicitly demonstrates that you are tired. By naming it and bringing it into your conscious reality, you have also compounded the feeling. Or if you find yourself experiencing the surge of joy and excitement that happens when you meet a new love, you'll soon tell yourself, 'I'm in love'. This statement will heighten your sensation and will connect you to the file in your brain called 'Ways to behave when I am besotted with someone'. Before you know it, you will start doing all the things you associate with being in love.

As we deepen our understanding of the subtleties of life, we have to learn more and more words to describe our experiences. When we name these experiences, we also magnify them and give them a life of their own. As a child I can remember sometimes feeling a certain type of discomfort that I eventually learned to call 'embarrassment'. Interestingly, once I had discovered the word to fit the feeling, I found myself starting to blush a lot more often. By naming it, I had made 'embarrassment' a separate entity that could of itself trigger my reactions, instead of the other way around. I found myself 'doing' embarrassment at the least stimulus because it had become an identifiable part of my emotional repertoire. Similarly, few people seemed to experience 'road rage' until one day somebody coined the phrase. Then suddenly there was road rage everywhere. When you name something you bring it firmly into your earth level reality.

Clearly then, language is a very powerful factor in your experience of the world. If you want to communicate your thoughts, feelings, needs and desires clearly and effectively, you must pay attention to the kind of words that you use. Just as with our belief systems, you must also be ever vigilant over the types of words and phrases that you allow into your mind. You need to create language for yourself that reflects your highest, most positive and spiritually fit self.

MAKING YOUR LANGUAGE A POWERFUL TOOL

As you start to develop these positive language patterns, you might first consider any disempowering ways in which you've been using language and how you can turn them around.

Why Gossip Hurts

One of our most negative uses of language happens when we gossip. This is very much an earth level way of communicating and it takes determined, conscious efforts on our part to stop, and focus instead on the positive aspects of people and situations. Of course, gossip is something that we all indulge in to one degree or another. I used to love to gossip and I sometimes still catch myself doing it when no one is listening! I'm not suggesting that you spend your life never mentioning another person in your conversation. In our daily discourse, we all talk about each other and this is perfectly natural. What is important is that you always try to come from a place of love and understanding when you do it.

A good way to turn this practice around is to understand how gossiping affects you energetically. When we get together with friends or co-workers and complain about the idiosyncrasies and failings of others, we create a fearful vortex of energy around us. For instance, have you ever had the experience of walking into a room only to find that conversation ceases and everyone turns to look at you in a rather guilty fashion? If so, you'll know how this type of energy feels. It is dark and heavy and the discomfort you experience comes from the negativity that has just been whipped up by the fear-based practice of gossiping.

Conversation is like a game of energy tennis – back and forth we go with our words, opinions and judgments until we manage to build up between us a whirlwind of bubbles of thought-energy. If you have been gossiping, these bubbles will be filled with the negative energy of your judgments. They will carry phrases like 'He couldn't give a damn about anyone but himself' or 'The trouble with her is that she thinks she knows it all' or 'He's so dysfunctional, he's completely out of touch with his feelings'. Remember that it is impossible to be judgmental towards someone without experiencing the negativity of that judgment in yourself. You can't gossip about a person and maintain feelings of serenity and unconditional love at the same time!

So why do we do it? Gossip is something most of us do when we are feeling vulnerable, separate from others and separate from our source. We try to bolster our fragile sense of self through the belief that making anyone else seem 'less' than us will automatically makes us feel stronger. Gossip is one of the great providers of a false sense of security. It also makes us think we are connecting with others on a heart level when in fact we are simply inviting them to join us in our world of fear-based perception.

In my Spiritual Fitness workout groups, one of our assignments is to avoid gossiping for a week. At first, people wonder what on earth they are going to talk about. When I first did this exercise, I thought I would have to be completely silent for seven days! In the end I enjoyed the practice so much I have made it an essential part of my life. It makes me feel lighter, stronger, wiser and much more compassionate. It has also improved all of my relationships – with those I would normally have gossiped about – because I now approach them without paranoia and judgment – and those I would normally have gossiped with – because we have to connect at a higher and deeper level. Instead of talking about the weaknesses of others, we are forced to confront our own. Instead of finding cause for complaint in everything around us, we have to seek out the worth and the beauty that is there.

I'm not suggesting that you never let off steam or voice your concerns to a friend if you feel someone has been treating you unfairly – there are times when we each of us need to use a friend as a sounding board to gauge the truth. Instead, make this a fruitful exercise by listening to yourself objectively as you talk. While the problem may be the result of your oppressor's personal issues, it may be that there is fault on your side! Take a soul level look at the situation, accept responsibility for any part you are playing in the scenario and then use it as an opportunity for learning and growth. Then go ahead and make the necessary changes that will improve the quality of your life.

To raise your level of conversation and communication with others, begin by cultivating within yourself the habit of looking for the good in people and making sure you express it *to* them and when talking *about* them. This is a very uplifting and rewarding experience. Remember that we are all doing the best we can in every moment. If you allow others to have their failings without judging them, you will notice your relationship with them begin to improve. You'll also start to feel better about yourself as you develop increasing integrity.

Dealing with Arguments

Another negative use of language occurs when we argue. If you watch or feel the negative energy between two people arguing, you will notice it bounce back and forth. Angry words are like punches but, just like boxing jabs, only a few are accurate enough to make a definite impact. When you argue, the heightened state of emotion caused by your anger tends to move you away from the centre of your authentic self.

Much of the time you are not saying things you truly mean or, if you are, you're speaking from the distorted perception of your fearful self. Remember again that at the basis of all emotions there are really only two – fear and love. Since anger doesn't fit into the love category, then it must be the product of fear.

The best way to deal with someone who is attacking you verbally is to change the rhythm and tone of the exchange. If they raise their voice, then lower yours. If they are gesticulating madly, then keep your body as still as possible. Most importantly, remember that all attack is a cry for help. This belief will alter your actions and, ultimately, your experience. If your attacker is someone you know well, then disengage from the fight and try responding to them with the question, 'What is it that you are actually afraid of?' For a moment this may appear to confuse them and take the wind out of their sails, since they may not be aware that behind their anger is fear. Yet, if they are prepared to consider the implications of this question, you should soon see the anger dissolve as the real issue that is driving them rises to the surface.

If you are dealing with someone who you don't know so well, you can soften the confrontation simply by interrupting the flow of abuse. Do something unexpected and it will immediately start to diffuse the situation. For example, bend down to tighten your shoelace, move out of their field of vision or sit down if you are standing up. If you think you can get away with it, you could do something comically outrageous such as performing a little dance! If you imagine how you would distract an upset child, this should give you some idea of how to deal with an angry person.

Harsh words are the echoes of our frightened selves. Like gossip they say more about our own state of mind than they do about the person they are aimed at. Since all words are actually sounds and symbols of energy, harsh words interfere with your vibration and contaminate your psyche. One of the most powerful actions that you can take on your road to Spiritual Fitness is to eliminate as much aggressive, negative talk from your reality as possible – not only by eradicating yours, but also by not engaging with that of others.

As you become more sensitive and spiritually fit, you will begin to understand what people are saying without listening to the actual words they are speaking. You will be able to tell by their intonation, the timbre or pitch of their voice, what they are trying to communicate to you. If they are attacking you, your open and loving heart will enable you to be compassionate and understanding enough to stay calm and not take the attack personally. Then you will be able to respond to them in your own subliminal way. As much by what you do not say as by the words you utter, by your body language, intonation, facial expression and general demeanour, you will emit an energy that says, 'It's okay, you are safe with me. I am not here to judge you but to ease your way forward in any way that I can.' You will soon find that with little conscious effort you are able to soothe and console others both with the words that you use and the spaces in between them.

Making Love Your Only Four-Letter Word!

Based on the principle of the power of language, we have learnt that swearing, cursing and hurling torrents of verbal abuse cannot possibly make you feel good! Not only are they the products of unbalanced, fearful emotions, they also carry the energy of anger and hatred that is so damaging to your soul. I can remember that I always used a string of four-letter expletives whenever I felt threatened in some way. At the time I didn't know that, far from helping me to feel better, the bitter words I was spitting out were actually leaving their own bitter taste in my mouth. As I have learned to curb my abusive language, I have found myself feeling much calmer and more loving.

Of course, after years of exposure to outside influences, much of our 'bad' language has become automatic. Sometimes it provides an emphatic way for us to get our point across and, as long as you use it sparingly and only for extreme self-expression, you'll find it won't pollute your consciousness. Soon you'll feel a lot lighter, cleaner and more positive.

Avoiding Self-criticism

As well as learning to speak to (and about) others with generosity and compassion, you must also become aware of the way that you talk to yourself. Most of us spend a lot of our time scaring ourselves senseless with the things that we say to ourselves. We have many different voices in our heads that seem to appear from all directions and present themselves to us in a devastatingly critical fashion. Some of them are openly aggressive, some are panicky and some can be deceptively seductive in their suggestions.

You might like to take a moment to identify some of these voices for yourself. For example, think for a moment of a situation that scares you …

Now notice the kind of voice that is suddenly talking inside your head …

Is it fast and breathless, scare-mongering and sensationalist? This is the type of voice that says, 'Well just how do you think you're going to pay the bills, what with the way you keep spending *and* then there are all the debts you already have and how do you think you are going to earn more money anyway because before you know it you are going to be completely bankrupt and end up in the gutter?' Or you may have a slow, ponderous voice that says, 'You don't have a hope of achieving your goals. Look at you; what talents do you really have?'

Start by recognizing this voice for what it really is – that of a deeply frightened aspect of your being that is desperately trying to get you to avoid your own greatness, (for all the reasons we saw in WorkOut One). You can then do one of several things – whichever feels the best and most appropriate for you. You can sit quietly and reason with it, in the same way as you would with someone who is verbally attacking you. You can deflect its power and get to the root of the matter by asking this frightened voice what it is really afraid of. You'll discover that it actually believes it is helping you by warning or protecting you. Continue a dialogue with this voice until it is prepared to allow you to take some new steps forward. Acknowledge its basic need to feel safe and promise to consult it every step of the way to make sure that it feels comfortable. After all, it simply needs your reassurance that you know what you're doing and that everything will be OK.

Another approach is to regard your fearful voice in a more abstract fashion and treat it as a disembodied voice inside your head, much like the voice you hear coming from a radio. Extend this analogy and imagine you are turning it off, fading it into the background or changing stations until you hear something that is more appealing to you. You might like to try this now to see how effective this approach is for you.

Alternatively, instead of turning the noise off, you can try drowning out this fearful voice by continuously reciting a positive mantra, either silently or out loud to yourself, along the lines of 'I am peace' or 'I am courage'. (We will be looking at mantras again later in this WorkOut).

Beyond your frightened voice, there is the more insidious one that tries to seduce you into being less than you are. Do you recognize the voice that says, 'Go on, one more drink, drug or piece of junk food really won't do you any harm'? Or it may try to persuade you to put off chasing your dreams until another day and instead just sit around in the numbing paralysis of inaction. I knew a man who was reduced to a childlike state of helplessness in this way whenever he considered a bold, new scheme. It's usually quite pointless trying to reason with this voice because it is in denial about its root fear. It comes from the part of you that has cultivated a powerful bravado to hide its terror. Instead you must firmly assert yourself over it. It is the voice to which you 'just say no'.

You can apply these principles to all the negative voices that speak to you – those that anger or sadden you, those that criticize you for not doing better and even those that tell you that you are better than anyone else. Learn to recognize your disempowering voices and treat them as you would any other negative influences – with soul level awareness and firmness.

When you have done this you can seek out the one voice that is there to guide and support you at all times. This is the voice of your higher self, or the voice of the universal intelligence, as it speaks inside you. In WorkOut Five we will look at how you can dialogue with this voice through the stillness and silence of meditation. For now, just trust this voice is available to you and get a sense of what it sounds like. It may manifest as the voice of your intuition or a sudden insight. It may be the voice that puts a comforting thought inside your head to ease your tears. Or it may be the voice that rejoices with you in your triumphs and helps you to feel exhilarated. Most of the time I find that this voice seems to speak from *inside* me rather than at me, coming from deep within my being. And on other occasions, for example, when I'm receiving intuitive information about people, this voice seems to come in through my right ear. Whatever form it takes, you will come to recognize this voice of the universal life force by the fact that it makes you feel genuinely good about yourself whenever you listen to it.

Developing Positive Self-talk

As you become aware of the power of your language, you can start to tailor it to suit your needs. To do this, first think of some of the everyday expressions that you use. For example, when someone asks you how you are, do you reply with 'Not too bad', 'Okay, thank you' or 'Fine'? ('Fine' is one of the words that we have learned to use to keep the world at bay. It means very little and is often used as a stock answer that actually says, 'Don't ask me any more questions'). Try some more positive responses such as 'Wonderful' or 'Doing very well, thank you.' As you hear yourself speak the words, you will instantly feel good about yourself.

And when there is something that you really want to do, how do you express this to the world? Do you say 'I'm trying to' or 'I'm hoping to'? Remember that the universal life force will mirror the strength of your desires. If you really want to get the maximum benefit from the powerful energies that surround you, start saying 'I am going to' or 'I am planning to' or even better, talk about your dreams as if they are already coming true!

In one of the exercises I use in my Spiritual Fitness WorkOut Groups, I interview the group members about their dreams *as if they have already achieved them.* We call this playing 'Oprah' and, as in that inspiring show, I ask them to tell me exactly how they went about making their dreams a reality. As each story unfolds, an almost palpable energy shift takes place as each person recognizes the magical power within. As one woman discussed how she had 'already created' her dream of owning a successful country hotel retreat, she found herself coming up with detailed ideas for it that previously hadn't occurred to her. By naming their talents and describing their passage to power, each participant in this exercise uses the power of the spoken word to create a template inside their heart and mind for future success.

Another good language technique to develop is known as 'positive reframing'. This entails re-writing the script of your life from a soul level angle. Doing this forces you to find the sense of meaning that we all long for. Instead of referring to the 'problems' and 'obstacles' in your life, you can start to describe them as 'invitations'. This harnesses the universal life force that is encouraging you to move forward and grow. So, if you're experiencing financial difficulties, instead of saying 'I'm broke', you can start to tell people that it's clearly time for you to use your unique talents to make some extra money. As you begin to define your life in this more upbeat fashion, it will take on the shape and hue of your more positive perception. If you do this with the genuine conviction of your heart, you'll find your life experiences soon improving.

You will also need to pay attention to the way that you discuss events that have saddened or angered you. When we are feeling any extreme emotion we all have a tendency to want to share it with others. How many times have you got on the phone and repeated the same story over and over to a succession of friends, with the sole aim of soliciting commiseration? At these times we are not interested in soul level thinking. We don't want to know what is the potential lesson for us here. We just want to have our sorry tales heard as an acknowledgment of how justifiably bad we're feeling. This may provide a temporary feeling of consolation but you must realize that this type of interaction never helps your situation. Whenever you insist on discussing your experiences purely in a negative light, it only serves to compound your feelings of helplessness.

Instead, you may like to start to cultivate the kind of friends who will help you be more constructive in your thinking and conversation; the sort of friends who can share a soul level perspective with you. If you think you don't yet know anyone like that, then stand your ground and think that way for yourself. As you become more positive and a living example of soul level thinking, your calmness and insight will interest those who aren't there yet and also draw to you a whole new set of people who are. Before you know it, you'll be a beacon of inspiration to all those around you and have plenty of friends with whom you can share your experiences in a positive way.

Saying What You Mean and Meaning What You Say

Having looked at some of our more complex uses of language, let's remember that the two most powerful words you have at your disposal are 'yes' and 'no'. So many of our interactions contain our roundabout ways of trying to express these two basic words! We all know how this goes. Someone asks you to an event that holds no appeal to you but you're afraid of hurting their feelings by saying an outright 'no'. So you take a circuitous route and invent an elaborate story as to why you can't go – your distant relatives are flying in from Outer Mongolia; the plumber is due *any* time in the next two weeks; or you have to paint your house before winter arrives!

Lying is the most unhealthy use of language that we ever engage in. From a white lie to a barefaced lie, if you are at all self-aware you can never feel good when you lie. This is because lying interferes with your natural energy flow and throws you out of sync with the actuality of life. As the old saying goes, 'The truth shall set you free', but untruths will fix you in a place of non-alignment. Whenever you are trying to convince others of something that you actually know to be untrue, you are not being 'straight', (meaning 'direct'), and the energy around you becomes confused and heavy. Sooner or later this will reflect in your inner being and make you feel bad about yourself at a deep level.

Unless we are pathological liars, for most of us the hardest lies to avoid, (and perhaps the only lies we tell), are 'white' lies. These are the ones we tell when we believe that to do so is somehow making the situation better for all concerned. For example, you don't want to upset or disappoint someone, so you pretend you weren't feeling well when you failed to show up for their party, or say that you overslept when you deliberately missed an engagement with them. These lies may seem innocuous enough and you may wonder what could really be the harm in such behaviour. I would say that this depends on the level of Spiritual Fitness that you want to achieve. If you wish, you can go through the rest of your life pacifying and pleasing others with seemingly harmless half-truths. On an earth level this will do the job nicely and everybody will leave happy and sleep comfortably in their beds at night. But if you feel ready to take a soul level approach to this issue, then only truth will do.

If you choose to take this approach, then start by asking yourself who you really think you are helping by not being completely honest. The answer will usually be 'yourself', because you are trying to avoid any potential awkwardness. Instead, remember that one of our soul level aims in life is to help each other grow and this means being courageous, loving and honest. As you become more sensitive to the energy you create through your communication, you will quickly discover that the most painless and most satisfying way to communicate is by being absolutely truthful. Your enhanced sense of compassion will help you to find the right way to say what you mean with love, diplomacy and humour. And your relationships will grow closer as people come to rely on you as someone they can trust for an honest and constructive opinion.

Walking Your Talk

Of course, learning how to say 'yes' and 'no' means a lot more than not lying. These words are a powerful expression of your sense of self, of self-worth and self-love. They force you to have confidence in your decisions. This means that you must know and trust yourself enough to be able to make decisions based on your heart's truth. For example, despite peer pressure, do you really want to say 'no' to spending the weekend with your work mates on a team-building exercise because your heart knows you need to spend more time with your partner and children? Or do you dream of expressing your hidden creative talents, but never stand up to be counted by simply saying 'yes' whenever the opportunity arises? Learning to speak from your authentic self will help you make huge strides towards personal freedom, happiness and Spiritual Fitness.

In order to 'walk your talk' with conviction you need two basic beliefs. One is that what you want in life is justified, that you deserve to get your needs and desires met. The other is that you don't have to do things you don't want to do. If, for instance, you no longer wish to cover for lazy co-workers or do every last scrap of housework yourself despite having an able-bodied partner, then it's up to you to gather up your feelings of self-worth and say a firm 'no'. Or, if you get the chance to do something that you've always wanted to do, such as, say, scuba diving or travelling around the world, be ready to manifest your desires by just saying 'yes'. Remember that the world will only take you as seriously as you take yourself. If you say 'yes' or 'no' with enough conviction and stick to your guns, then your reality will begin to change around you to meet your deepest needs.

As you become more aligned with your language, you'll feel your personal power starting to grow. On the other hand, if you are forever going back on your word and making wild statements that you never keep to then your spirit will begin to weaken. If, for example, every time you have a disagreement with someone you declare that you are 'never going to speak to them again', you might like to check with yourself whether this is a realistic statement. Are you really never, ever going to utter one word to them again? Similarly, do you constantly claim that you will 'never again' touch alcohol, cigarettes or junk food, only to find yourself indulging in them shortly afterwards? As you become more honest with yourself, you'll understand the difference between unrealistic, dramatic resolutions that are guaranteed to fail, and powerful declarations of intent that will force you to stretch into a new reality. You will start to walk your talk and you will find your self-esteem growing daily.

Using Powerful Phrases

In your increasingly conscious use of language, you will soon discover how to construct your phraseology for maximum effect. In some modern spiritual traditions much credence is given to the power of affirmations. This can mean jumping out of bed in the morning and reciting parrot fashion (preferably to your mirror image) phrases such as 'I am beautiful', 'I am strong', 'I am wealthy', and so on. While no energy work is ever completely wasted and these affirmations can make you feel better, there is a way of making positive statements to yourself and the universe that is much more powerful and effective.

Mantras have been used in the east for many centuries and have a proven history of transformational power. In their purest form they are simply one word or sound, but I have discovered that the mantra 'I am', followed by any positive abstract noun, is an extremely powerful way of using language. So, for example, it is much more powerful to use the phrase 'I am peace' rather than the phrase 'I am peaceful', or 'I am strength' instead of 'I am strong'. Try saying each of these four phrases, one at a time, slowly and out loud. Pause between each and, as you do, notice the impact that their vibration has inside you. You will begin to feel their different powers echoing around your whole being. On your in-breath declare 'I am' in your strongest, most resonant voice and on the out-breath follow with the word 'peaceful'. Now repeat this but this time substitute the word 'peace' for 'peaceful'. You'll probably notice that when you use the noun, as in 'I am peace', this has a much greater effect on you than when you use the adjective, as in 'I am peaceful'. This is because adjectives are merely descriptions that serve to distance you from a state by forcing you to observe and define it. Yet when you use a noun, you are identifying with the concept and become more at one with it. (In WorkOut Five we shall look at how you can harness the power of mantras by incorporating them into your meditation).

This process also works in reverse. If you want to lessen the effect of negative statements, you can move one step further away from 'I am' plus an adjective and use the phrase 'I am' with a verb. You will move away from the absoluteness of 'I am sadness', through the observation of 'I am sad' to the most distant of all, 'I am experiencing sadness'. This gives you the message that you are not your emotions but are simply passing through them. Try saying these three phrases out loud now, in rhythm with your breath, and notice the difference in their effects.

Eliminate the Negative, Accentuate the Positive

Finally, another powerful way to use language is by avoiding negative statements as much as possible. For example, instead of saying 'I don't want to eat junk food,' turn this into a positive statement by saying, 'I only want to eat healthy foods'. This device works because your subconscious mind automatically creates images, sounds and/or feelings for all the concepts it is given. When your subconscious hears 'I don't want to eat junk food' it gets busy summoning up the concept of 'junk food' without necessarily recognizing the positive motive behind your statement.

For example, if I tell you not to think of pink giraffes your mind first has to conjure up a concept of pink giraffes to be able to erase it. First, your subconscious mind rapidly searches through the files in your brain to form an image to attach to this idea, then your conscious mind moves in to eliminate it. No matter how quickly this occurs, you are still left with an imprint of pink giraffes on your subconscious mind. Similarly, if someone repeatedly tells you, 'Don't forget to pick up the dry-cleaning', the first command that filters through to your more powerful, subconscious mind is the word 'forget'. Before you can think about *not* forgetting you have to register with yourself what the concept of 'forgetting' means. This puts you into a forgetful state and before you know it, you're on your way home without the dry-cleaning.

If you learn to use your language in a conscious fashion, it will become an elegant and effective tool at your disposal. Begin to make your phrases direct and simple and keep them as positive as possible. 'Don't forget to pick up the dry-cleaning' can simply become 'Remember to pick up the dry-cleaning'; 'I don't want to get so stressed' can become 'I'm going to slow down and relax'. Your subconscious mind will grasp the concept much more easily, transmute it into a belief and before you know it, it will be manifesting as your reality.

Demystifying New Age Language

Much of this WorkOut has been dedicated to a left-brain, logical examination of your language patterns. Let's end with a more light-hearted, creative look at some of the so-called 'New Age' language that you may encounter on your path to Spiritual Fitness. Each culture has its own language that serves to separate it from all others, and different sections of society have their own jargon that can be similarly exclusive. For example, the language of the computer world, all 'megabytes', 'drives' and 'downloads', is quite unintelligible to the outsider. New Age jargon, a mixture of psychobabble, mystical vagueness and science fiction, can be equally confusing to the uninitiated.

One of the things that struck me when I first encountered New Age language was that some of the words and phrases seemed to be new euphemisms for old patterns of behaviour, while others were genuinely refined interpretations that provided me with a new perspective. For example, nobody seemed to have 'problems' any more – instead they all had 'challenges'. People didn't wake up in a bad mood, they were simply 'processing' their 'stuff' or 'issues'. There was much talk of 'embracing your shadow', which roughly translated means 'own up when you have a negative thought and stop giving yourself a hard time about it, because everyone else has them too'. (I later discovered that we also often 'embrace our shadow' when we decide to learn our lessons by doing all the things that are deemed 'bad' for us).

The phrase that confused me the most was the ubiquitous 'let it go'. This was one of my least favourites because I could never work out ex- actly what it meant. The less I understood it, the more life presented me with problems or, should I say, 'challenges', causing everyone to echo, 'let it go'. It seemed to be the universal remedy for everything – a blanket term with no particular meaning. It also seemed to be equally applicable to negative and positive experiences. If your relationship fell apart, you could just 'let it go'. If you really wanted a job/house/car, you just had to focus on it once and then 'let it go'.

In the end I came to understand this phrase to mean 'let it flow'. Everything has an optimum, most effective and natural course to follow which is for your highest good. If your relationship isn't working, give it your best effort and then 'let it go/flow' along that course. If you have money worries, use all the resources and creativity available to you and then 'let it go/flow' so that all avenues of possibility can open up to you. If your heart is set on a dream job, give it your best shot and then 'let it go/flow'. When you can sit back, let go and allow this natural course to unfold and flow, you will also be able to make a lot more sense out of apparently senseless situations.

Another interesting piece of New Age jargon is the term 'resonates'. I deciphered it in this way. Human beings, like all life forms, are in a constant state of flux. When one is sad, another is happy, when one is angry, another is loving. For us all to get along, we must be in a state of harmony. Of course, this doesn't mean that we all have to be in exactly the same mood at the same time but it does mean that we can reveal *parts* of ourselves that are sympathetic to those being revealed by the people around us. For example, if you are sad, then I can use my happiness to radiate support and love towards you. If you are angry, then I can stay calm and compassionate. So, to 'resonate' with someone literally means to 'strike a chord' of understanding with them. It can also mean meeting someone you feel is on your wavelength and feeling instantly close to them.

Whichever way you react to this language, the most important thing is that in your self-expression, you use the words and phrases that best describe what you truly feel. If the jargon works for you, then sprinkle it into your conversation and, if not, stay with words and expressions that feel most authentic to you. Your words weave a magic spell around you, (pun intended!), and can be used elegantly to improve the quality of your life. However you choose to use your language, become conscious of the effect that it has on you. As with your beliefs and your emotions, when you clean up and take control of the words inside your head, your outer world will begin to reflect your growing inner strength and Spiritual Fitness.

REVIEW

Language is one of the primary ways that we connect with the world around us and define its meaning. The way we describe life helps to direct the way we feel about it. Therefore we need to become conscious of our language patterns.

Negative language, such as gossip, arguments, self-criticism and lies, echoes inside us and makes us feel bad. Positive language, including constructive self-talk, mantras and the way we report our experiences to others, helps us to feel good and create a more positive reality. Learning to say 'yes' and 'no' authentically helps us recognize our heart's truth.

Only use New Age language if it makes sense to you!

THE INNER WORKOUT

1   Avoid all gossip, (giving and receiving), for the next week. Notice how this makes you feel lighter. It will also improve the quality of your relationships and sense of inner peace.

2   Pay attention to your use of negative language and replace it with positive expressions that have the same meaning, for example, 'I don't want to stay in bed all day' becomes 'I'm getting up early'.

3   Use the phrase 'I am experiencing' to describe your unwanted states and 'I am' plus a noun to identify your positive ones, for example, 'I am experiencing frustration' and 'I am happiness'.

4   Stop swearing so much! You'll feel a lot calmer.

5   Pay attention to the phrases that you use as part of your everyday language and weed out any disempowering expressions. For example, if your answerphone message starts with 'I'm afraid there's no one here at the moment', you can quickly drop the 'I'm afraid', (unless of course you think your machine is genuinely frightened of being alone).

Consciously use empowering statements whenever you are speaking about yourself and your needs and desires.

6 Give yourself a 'word bath'. Pick up a thesaurus and look up one of your favourite positive words. Then read out loud all the other definitions of it. As you recite each word, you will feel more and more uplifted. You might like to begin with 'happiness'. Take a moment now to recite the following words out loud and notice how great you feel afterwards:

joy, pleasure, thrill, rapture, delight, euphoria, laughter, exhilaration, enjoyment, exaltation, fun.

7 Get together with some friends and, instead of gossiping, play 'Oprah'. Take it in turns to interview each other as if your dreams are already a reality and surprise yourself by revealing the inner resources you already have.

THE RELATIONSHIP EQUATION

**'Love is not looking into one another's eyes
but looking together in the same direction.'**

Antoine de Saint-Exupéry

So far we have looked at life mainly from an earth level approach. We have examined how you can direct the more conscious aspects of your thought processes to work in your best interests. Now, at the halfway point in this course, we can begin to explore more of a soul level approach. You can start to view everything in the context of a much bigger, overall picture and to discover deeper reasons for the events in your life. You can then learn to use this new understanding to make your life more joyful and rewarding.

In the previous WorkOut we looked at language as one of the ways in which we fulfil our deep need for connection. This week we can go deeper and ask what this connection with others really means to us and why it is so necessary for our soul's growth and Spiritual Fitness.

WHAT IS THIS THING CALLED LOVE?

When we enter into an intimate relationship with another person, by sleeping alongside each other, making love with each other and spending time together, we absorb a great amount of each other's energies. Soon these overflow and merge to form a separate entity between us that becomes our 'relationship'. This entity takes on a life of its own and, when we are under its influence, we will often engage in some of our most outrageous and irrational behaviour! At other times this entity will produce in us some of our noblest actions. In this WorkOut let's look at why we create this unique entity in our lives and explore how, by understanding it from a soul level perspective, we can find in our relationship deep love, joy, wisdom and support on our life's path.

The Urge to Connect

'Can't live with them and can't live without them' is the refrain that most of us have echoed about romantic relationships at some time in our lives. Yet no matter how difficult we have found our partnerships in the past, we still continue to seek out or engage with that special someone, who we feel will somehow fulfil our lives. Even those who say they have been so hurt that they will never again enter into a relationship, usually have an inner world filled with romantic memories or fantasies, in which they seek solace. We are all driven by a deep urge to form an intimate connection with the world around us and most of us choose to do this through relationships. Before you can begin to have a successful relationship, you need to be honest about what it is that you're actually hoping to get from one. If you take a soul level look at this, you will see that your need for partnership actually stems from your basic human need to overcome your earthly sense of separation.

To understand this desire better, you'll first need to trace your soul's journey back to its arrival on this earth. When you first came into this world it was as if you had been dropped in by parachute with no map.

You arrived in a foreign land and were surrounded by strange talking heads. Everything was new and it seemed that the only people who could help you were the ones you found around you. You arrived with no opinions about life and were open to all the suggestions of others. You started off with a naturally joyful nature and a loving little heart to match. Yet, as you began to spend more time with your guardians on earth, you may have noticed that they seemed a lot less joyful than you. In fact, most of the time they seemed to be in the grip of earth level, fear-based thinking. You may have heard them talk about other people, or groups of people, in a negative way. Or they may have repeatedly warned you about the dangers of living in this world. Gradually, some of their fearful thinking seeped into your consciousness and you came to notice that it didn't make you feel good. In fact it made you feel frightened and alone and suspicious of others. As a very small child you'd been happy to trust and connect with everyone around you, but now you felt less safe and started to dream of just one person who could comfort you and make you feel safe again. Uncertain of who you could trust, you secretly yearned for someone just like you, in the hope that they could help you get back to your naturally joyful nature.

It was at this point that you began your soul's real mission on earth: that is, to overcome the illusion of separation that we all feel, and join with each other in love, instead of avoiding each other out of fear. Only in this loving connection can we find lasting peace and real happiness. Our job is to help one another to find our way back 'home' to our original loving and open state. Somewhere in your soul's memory you can remember this home as the place where you are not defensive, where you can allow your heart to melt into tenderness, trust, love and hope. You long for this state again. The point of our lives, as far as I have been able to gauge it, is for us to learn to recreate this 'home' here on earth, wherever we are and whoever we are with.

So, it is this urge to return to your most natural state, to how you first felt when you arrived on this planet, which gives you an overwhelming need for connection. It reflects your yearning for your infinite self. In turn, the fear and confusion you have since absorbed have convinced you the only way to reach your 'home' again is by entering into an intimate relationship with just one person. Your fear also tells you that by connecting with just one person, you might still have some control over the levels of trust, openness and defencelessness that will be demanded of you.

This whole concept creates one of the first obstacles on your path to a successful partnership. It is unfair and unrealistic to look for your lost sense of infinity in another person, especially since they have most likely lost theirs too. If you are looking for joy and wholeness then first look inside yourself and reconnect with the power that originally gave them to you – the universal life force that created you. For your intimate relationship to be successful, you will both need to develop your own spiritual connection. You'll need to realize that what you each need in order to make you whole is to be found in yourselves and not in one another. You are together to support one another on your mutual journeys. This way you can make your union an exciting adventure on which you both quest your naturally loving and open state together, instead of in each other. This will form a powerful, loving and fulfilling bond between you.

Of course, all of our human interactions with each other are to some degree 'relationships'. If you are seeking intimacy, trust and open-heartedness only through romantic relationships, then this not only puts a tremendous pressure on your partner but also undervalues your connection with your family, friends and co-workers. When I first learned this basic truth it forced me to open up my authentic self to the world around me instead of hiding it in a romantic relationship and unrealistically expecting my partner to fulfil all my needs. To have successful romantic relationships, you need to begin by developing authentic, heartfelt connection with *everyone* you know. This doesn't mean you have to kiss the bus driver or tell your boss your deepest secrets, but, instead, that you do not hide who you are in your dealings with others. As you start to speak your truth and express your real needs and desires to those around you, you will instantly start to experience the sense of connection that you crave.

Soul Level Relationships versus Earth Level Relationships

Before we go any further and examine specific relationship issues, it's essential that you equip yourself with your most powerful tool for understanding relationships, which is soul level thinking. It is also useful to bear in mind at this stage that the soul level way of looking at a relationship and the earth level approach to one are often completely contradictory! This is because the earth level is based on fear and the soul level sees only real love and truth. So, if your partner is causing you to experience earth level pain, on a soul level they're actually giving you a wonderful opportunity to heal a fearful part of yourself. Do you, for example, feel bereft whenever they are away from you and do you seem unable to find happiness in your own company? It is at these times that, on a soul level, you are in fact being invited to (re)discover your own strength, your own importance and vitality.

I often hear people say that when their relationship ended, they felt as if their life ended with it. I reply to them that *on a soul level* this was the very reason that their relationship had to end in the first place. Our relationships are not meant to take away our sense of personal power or resourcefulness. Nor are they supposed to make us feel unable to enjoy life on our own. If you allow your inner light to become so dim that it cannot exist on its own, then on a soul level your lover leaving you is the most loving thing that they can do for you, no matter how much this may at first hurt you *on an earth level*. At this level, your lover's departure may be a terrible thing, leaving you with all sorts of problems such as extra bills, no home or a seemingly broken heart. Yet, no matter what earthly predicament the loss of a relationship may cause, in the end only soul level thinking can console and uplift you because it reveals to you the highest truth of the situation.

Soul level thinking shows us the meaning of real love. It teaches us that every partner is the 'right' one in some way – providing that we are able to discover their real gift to us. A powerful belief you can adopt is to trust that before you enter into any relationship, your two souls make an agreement to teach each other what they most need to learn. (This of course can't be made known to your more earthbound sides or the strategy wouldn't work.) In this way, you can finally learn to transcend the fears that this earth level version is based on.

For example, imagine that your soul needs to work on expressing creativity in this lifetime, but that this is also your deepest fear. You may then agree in advance that your partner will make the *pain* of your lack of creativity so intense that it becomes greater than your actual *fear* of being creative. As we saw in WorkOut One, when the pain of where you are becomes greater than your actual fear of leaving it, you will finally take action. So, they will endlessly taunt you for your apparent lack of creative ability until they eventually light the touch paper inside you that will cause you to flare up into your magnificently creative self. Or, if you need to work on self-assertion, they may bully you mercilessly until you're finally so battered that one day you suddenly overcome your fear and stand up for yourself to relieve the pressure of your pain.

A woman once came to me who was devastated by the loss of her relationship. She was experiencing a lot of emotional pain, caused by the fact that her lover had left and moved in with one of her friends. Her thinking had become stuck in an earth level loop and all that she could think of was how to hurt him back, believing that this would ease her pain. I broke her out of this loop by asking her some soul level questions. They were, 'What are you now able to do with your life that you couldn't do in this relationship? Who was the person you were afraid to be that this break-up has now unleashed in you?' After thinking for some time, she realized that, since the end of her relationship, she had begun to turn to her previously suppressed spirituality. She was starting to meditate and find the voice of the strong, intuitive woman inside her which had been kept quiet for so long. Over the next few months I watched her develop her Spiritual Fitness until she found peace in her heart by understanding the soul gifts her former lover had given her. She was able to assimilate the lessons of their souls' agreement and has now opened her own spiritual centre and become a gifted healer.

So, earth level reality and soul level reality sometimes have to be diametrically opposed. By prior agreement, the deep soul love that you share with your partner may be unable to reveal itself in your everyday reality so that it can work most effectively. Instead you may experience great pain. At this point you must also remember that for the duration of your stay on this planet, your human existence is as valid as your soul's existence. You do not have to stay in any relationship that threatens your safety or demeans you in any way. At these times, your partner's gift to you is to show you how to walk away from anything that doesn't honour your highest good.

Soul level thinking will also enable you to learn (and teach) your relationship lessons as quickly as possible, and it will prevent you or another from having to repeat this pain. As with much soul level activity, it may take time for you to perceive the true value of every situation. Like everything else, your spiritual awareness will strengthen with practice, until seeing the positive opportunities in every situation comes naturally to you. You'll then be able to act swiftly and effectively to accept these opportunities for growth into your life and your relationships will be much more enjoyable and rewarding.

HOW TO GET THE BEST FROM YOUR RELATIONSHIPS

As we learnt in WorkOut One, two of our greatest motivators for change and personal growth are despair and desire. Since romantic relationships hold the potential for both of these, they naturally become

major areas of soul development for us. It is precisely because our relationships often bring up such intense emotions in us that they often
make our thinking unclear. So, let's stop and consider some of the facts.
These facts are so true for us all that you can, if you like, think of them
as the universal 'laws' of romantic relationships. For our relationships to
be successful, they must adhere to these laws and contain the following
three qualities.

The Three Laws of Successful Relationships

I SELF-LOVE

The first fact is that it's impossible for you to connect with someone
else's heart if you haven't yet connected with your own. All heart connection is a two-way affair and, for it to work, it needs *two* heart centres
that are open and able to feel love. Until you connect with your own
centre and feelings, any partner who reaches out to you will find that
there is nothing there for them to connect with. For example, if your
partner wants to open up their heart and be vulnerable with you, but
you have not yet learned to open up your heart and be vulnerable
yourself, you will not be able to receive this gift from them. You won't
be able to find any frame of reference inside you that will enable you
to understand and deal with their emotions.

The greatest gift that you bring to your romantic relationships is
your honest and healthy relationship with yourself. To achieve this
you have to take responsibility for your emotions and learn to fulfil
your own needs. As you do so, your growing self-love will help you to
understand and soothe away your past hurts, feel more balanced in
your life and find greater joy in the world around you. Consequently,
you will no longer need your partner to be your healer, saviour or en-
tertainer. You will instead find a sense of completeness in yourself and
when you feel whole within yourself, you'll be able to approach your
relationship from the viewpoint of what you can bring to it rather than
what you need to take from it. This will automatically take a lot of

pressure off your partner and at the same time make you a million times more attractive to them! You will quickly discover that self-love is an essential ingredient in the recipe for any successful relationship.

2 RESPECT

It is a sad but true fact that when any of us enter into romantic relationships we engage in some of our most bizarre and outrageous behaviour. Despite claiming that we love our partner more than anyone else in the world, we frequently treat them in the most disrespectful of ways, ways in which we would not dream of treating our friends, family or co-workers. For example, you may be intolerant of your partner's life dreams, forever mocking and picking holes in them and constantly nagging your partner to be more 'realistic'. Yet, if your friends come to you with the same ideas, you may prove to be far more open to their plans and even offer to support them in their quest.

To prevent your relationship from falling into a pit of petty fault-finding and one-upmanship, you will need to develop respect for your partner and their soul's journey. This means standing back and allowing them to make their own mistakes and discoveries, while still providing them with a supportively strong and loving base. It does not mean getting on the phone and constantly complaining about their shortcomings to your friends! Judgments, expectations of how they should behave, or any attempts on your part to manipulate their behaviour, defile the sacredness of the journeys that you are both on together. They trap you in a self-limiting loop of earth level thinking and prevent you from experiencing your natural state of love and joy, which was the state you hoped to rediscover by entering the relationship.

Often, when people first reawaken to their spiritual path, they will try to force their partners to join them in their meditations, workshops or new diets. If your partner is reluctant to take these steps because they're not yet ready, to attempt to force them to do so is disrespectful. Part of the job of respecting your partner is to allow them to go at their own pace and learn their own lessons for themselves. If their soul has chosen to stop and experience the denser aspects of life then your part is simply to support and inspire them *by example only*. I have heard of many enlightened beings who have helped their partners to evolve simply by becoming more light and loving with them.

For your relationship to be successful, you'll need to connect at a soul level and respect the journeys of self-discovery that you are both on together. This will help you to understand that your main role is to love and support one another. Seeing your lover in this way, as your friend and ally, will enable you to relate to one another in a balanced, respectful and mutually empowering way.

3 FREEDOM

Another of our strange relationship patterns is that many of us equate romantic partnership with ownership. Instead of dealing with our own insecurities by taking control of ourselves, (as recommended by 'law' one), we mistakenly believe that we can ease our sense of helplessness by controlling our partners instead. And so we might find ourselves interrogating them about where they are off to, the company they keep or the amount of money that they spend.

This urge to control can be quite insidious and often takes the subtlest of forms. For example, one of the first things that we often do, once we have embarked on a potentially long-term relationship, is to try and quash the very qualities in our partners that attracted us to them in the first place. If, for example, you were first drawn to your lover because they were so charming, vivacious and the life-and-soul of the party, these will often be the very qualities that begin to irk you once you are in a relationship with them. You may find yourself accusing them of flirting when really they were just being their usual vibrant self. You do this because you fear that if these qualities made them attractive to you, they will make them attractive to other people. This activates your own lack of self-love and the insecure belief that who you are is not enough to keep your partner interested in you. Not only does this behaviour hinder your partner's growth but it also provides you with a convenient distraction from your own, and also from re-claiming your own greatness. By focusing on keeping your partner small you also keep yourself small.

Again, this is another earth level way of relating that needs a soul level approach. For your relationship to thrive you must both allow each other the space to grow and shine as individual beings on a path of evolution. When you start to celebrate your partner's strengths and virtues your open-hearted generosity will also instantly make you feel bigger and better. Admiring and encouraging the divine spark in each other will set you both free to blossom. As you do so, you will each discover new gifts to bring to your relationship that will keep it alive and make you feel liberated and fulfilled.

THE GAMES WE PLAY

With these three laws in mind, let's look at some of the particular games that we play in our romantic relationships. As we have seen, when we enter into relationships our souls may have quite a different agenda than our earth level selves. Guided as we are by the tremendous intelligence of the universal life force, we will be led to the person that actually offers us the very thing our soul needs. The gift from that person can take many forms, one of which is that they become a mirror for the issues that we need to work on.

Projection

The most obvious and widely accepted interpretation of 'everyone is a mirror' is that our partners are in some way embodying a part of our hidden selves. If you want to know how this applies to your relationship, then take a look at the part of your partner that annoys you the most. Since we hate in others what we fear is in ourselves, it will give you a pretty good idea of an aspect of yourself that you are choosing not to deal with directly. For example, do you ever castigate your partner for their untidiness, laziness or thoughtlessness, only to discover that left to your own devices you behave exactly the same? Similarly, do you constantly complain that your partner never expresses their true feelings, yet secretly know that this is a convenient smokescreen for the fact that you don't really want to take too close a look at your own?

When we embark on relationships our souls agree in advance on the lessons we both can learn. So, sometimes your partner will act out before your eyes a negative or hidden aspect of yourself that you may be suppressing. They might, for example, be extremely reckless with money. You then have a choice to respond to this situation from an earth level point of view or from a soul level angle. If you choose the former, you will end up having endless arguments over spending. Although you may eventually come to some agreement, you will usually find that in the end you have just papered over the cracks. However, if you choose a soul level angle, you will be forced to examine which part of *you* would actually like to be more carefree with money but doesn't dare to be?

I have often discovered that I was projecting my own unresolved fears onto others in my own relationships. For a while I had a string of partners who seemed unable to fully commit themselves to our relationship. As I became more spiritually aware, instead of haranguing them for this, I was forced to admit that they were simply reflecting the free spirit in me that I was afraid to express. Needless to say, this was a profound revelation and as I learned to let out the free spirit in me, it helped me become a lot more powerful and balanced in my future relationships. Interestingly, after I had come to terms with this hidden aspect of myself, I also stopped attracting to me the type of person whom I had needed to mirror this fear for me.

So it is that we often project our deepest fears onto our partners and by our soul's agreement, get them to act out our fears for us. Sometimes too, we will project our fantasies onto them in other convoluted attempts to avoid our own greatness. For example, you may have a partner behind whose power you hide your own. Perhaps you are forever singing their praises, saying how wonderful they are and implying that you have little to offer in comparison. I once met a man who had been severely depressed for many years. When I asked him what was good about his life, he replied that the only good part of it was his wife and then launched into a very adulatory description of her talents and abilities. I pointed out to him that while it was wonderful that he felt such love and admiration for her, he was in fact feeling this at some cost to himself. By focusing only on her strengths, he was allowing his own to pass him by. I suggested to him that he began to ask himself the questions 'Who am I?' and 'What do I want?' Within weeks his depression began to lift as he found the courage to surround himself with his own power and not hide behind that of his wife.

Wherever you go you will encounter this particular syndrome in the relationships of those who choose to stay at home and wilt while their partners go out into the world and shine. For years this was the traditional role of women, although there is now a growing number of men who are using their female partners' success as an excuse to avoid accessing their own power. For any of you who have bought into this drama, it is useful to remember that you will never be fulfilled by living vicariously. No matter how great your payoff appears to be, such as financial security or inflated social status, your soul has come to this world to make its own contribution and only in so doing will you be able to find true happiness. And once you make your contribution, you will be able to bring back to your relationship an added dimension of worthiness and value.

The basic premise of this part of the mirror principle is that the way your partner behaves and treats you reflects who you believe you are inside. If you have a partner who cherishes and respects you, who values your talents and encourages your personal growth, then this reflects your love and respect for yourself. If, on the other hand, you have a partner who belittles your abilities and who has no respect for

THE RELATIONSHIP EQUATION

your deepest needs and desires, then this is also a reflection of your own low opinion of them. So if you want a partner who will love and honour you then your best plan is to start by loving and honouring yourself.

Outer Dramas, Inner Struggles

If we look even deeper, we will see that 'everyone is a mirror' does not simply mean that if you feel angry you will bump into an angry person in the street. Nor does it mean that if your partner is jealous, you have a secret jealous streak that you are not confronting. There are many more far-reaching implications to this idea. One such is that, at a soul level, your whole life is simply an external, symbolic enactment of your inner workings. You manifest a cast of characters and situations in your life that actually reflect the myriad aspects of yourself and the internal dramas with yourself. It is often suggested, for example, that your repressed father can be seen as a symbol of the suppressed part of you, or your aggressive partner as an outer reflection of your own inner aggression. This also means that your *outer conflicts* with these people are the symbols, or mirrors, of the *inner conflicts* that are taking place inside you. Your awkward relationship with your repressed father is showing you how ill at ease you are with the part of yourself that you are suppressing. Your volatile relationship with your aggressive partner is mirroring your struggle with your own aggressive self. So, 'everyone is a mirror' also means that your relationships with others are 'mirrors' of your relationships with yourself.

Within your personality, you have many aspects of your being that are seeking to relate to one another. For example, regardless of your sex, you have archetypal 'masculine' and 'feminine' sides, which are stereotypes of your outgoing and introspective sides. Part of your soul's task is to learn to harmonize and align these many aspects of your personality until you can be restored to your authentic whole self. By acting out your own inner drama with you, those around you are offering you the opportunity to carry out this process, to heal your wounded aspects and bring them into balance with each other.

I recall a woman coming to see me who was in a relationship with a very domineering man. Although she appeared to be a strong personality herself, whenever she was around her partner she seemed to weaken and become overshadowed. Her continual complaint was that he did not allow her to shine and express the exuberant side of her nature, that he constantly put her down and thwarted her attempts to be vibrant and make intelligent observations. If we had taken an earth level approach to this, we could have sat for hours discussing how she could best combat his bullying and get her own voice heard. Yet to do this would have been missing out on the greater, more important part of the picture. Instead, taking the soul level approach, I asked her how this relationship was a mirror of her own attitudes to parts of herself. Could it be that this was a reflection of the inner struggle that went on inside her own head, such as when the stronger part of her had a good idea but the more frightened, overbearing part of her quashed it in an attempt to make her avoid her own greatness?

In responding to these struggles, we do ourselves and our relationship a huge disservice if we don't seek out the deeper, soul level teachings behind them. It is very easy for us to simply condemn our partners for their unreasonable behaviour instead of understanding that this is merely a soul level pointer to the work that we need to do on ourselves. It's only by accepting some responsibility for a situation and looking inside at your own inner relationships that you can truly heal and expand both yourself and your external relationships.

Sex as a Mirror

Since sex is just another part of the way that you express yourself in relationships and act out your inner reality, the easiest way to understand your sexual self is to look at it from a soul level perspective. What is happening in your sex life is a mirror of what is happening at the soul level of your relationship. For example, if one of you is continually dominant in bed, this may be an indication of what is going on below the surface in the rest of your relationship and it could be a reflection of a power struggle that is occurring between you. Similarly, if one of you is unresponsive or closed down during sex, then this is usually a reflection of the way that person actually feels throughout your relationship.

As we have already seen, the outer circumstances of your relationship occur so that you can understand, heal and expand your own inner self. If you want your sex life to improve then look at the messages its dynamics are trying to give you. What do they say about your underlying attitudes to your partner and yourself? As you begin to accept responsibility for the feelings sex brings up in you and seek out the great teachings that they offer you, your sexual union will become much more tender and fulfilling.

Soul Mates – Fact or Fiction?

Each part of our culture has its own myth of true love and romance. The incurably romantic will dream of meeting Prince Charming or Sleeping Beauty, the more pragmatic will hope to find Mr or Ms Right and the spiritually aspiring will pray to encounter their 'soul mate'. Many people, myself included, have begun their path to Spiritual Fitness by forming what they think is a new 'soul mate' type of relationship, because it is based on what appear to be spiritual principles and seems to be some kind of mystical union. Yet, despite being more open with our feelings and having all the right terminology at our disposal, (such as saying we are having a 'power struggle' instead of an 'argument'), we still end up dealing with the same old lust and insecurities now dressed up in bells, beads and psychobabble.

When you encounter your real soul mate, you will immediately experience the difference. A true soul mate connection is a very sacred union that will rock your soul to its foundations and bring you to the greatest levels of love and transformation that you may ever encounter. The generally accepted notion of what a soul mate is has various connotations attached to it that, on closer examination, often prove to be completely erroneous. One false apprehension is that this kind of relationship comes attached with a guarantee of longevity. In my experience, I can assure you that you are actually a lot less likely to walk off happily into the sunset with your soul mate than you are with any other person! This sad but true fact is a result of another of the relationship truism – that soul level relationships and earth level relationships are often diametrically opposed.

Your soul mate is the one who has dedicated their love for you to the highest purpose. This means that they have come into your life to help you to learn your most important lessons and to give your soul the greatest opportunity for growth, (as you have also come into their life for the same reason). Yet, as we saw in WorkOut One, we are creatures of habit who crave the apparent comfort of familiarity, and so growth does not necessarily come easily to us. In fact, until we surrender to our higher spiritual power, it is the thing that we resist the most. So, if your soul mate is the one who is forcing you to expand beyond your perceived limits into behaviour that is very unfamiliar to you, this is unlikely to be one of the smoothest earthly relationships!

A soul mate relationship often follows a certain pattern. You meet and have an instant, dynamic and intense connection. Because of the power of the passion between you, you begin stretching way beyond your usual boundaries. You find yourself considering major life changes, such as the ending of any other relationships or a change of home or career. The intensity of your desire for this other person accesses and activates extremes of emotion in you that you never knew you had. It forces you to open up in ways you had previously thought were closed to you.

As a result of these dramatic major changes, your deepest fears and insecurities are jolted to the surface. You can find yourself plumbing the depths of despair as suddenly as you scale the heights of ecstasy.

It's at this point that you are able to receive the true gifts of deep love that your soul mate is offering you. This is often the greatest opportunity of your life for you to burst through old limitations and advance the evolution of your soul in leaps and bounds. For example, you may be given the chance to explore the deep wounds of a sense of abandonment and isolation that you have been carrying throughout this lifetime. Or you may be being invited to overcome low self-esteem and become the authentically powerful person that you have avoided in yourself for longer than you know.

Whatever the reason, meeting your soul mate will be one of the most challenging experiences of your life. In this other person you will recognize parts of yourself that you have both shunned and craved. As with all relationships, it is only by accepting responsibility for yourself and employing real understanding and total self-honesty that you will gain the true benefit of this union. You may find yourself feeling extremes of jealousy, rage or inadequacy and your task is to use these as tools to heal and rid yourself of the illusory fears that lie behind them.

On the more positive side, (yes, there is one!), your soul mate offers you the chance to love in a way that touches upon infinity. When you experience this deep level of love, life's rules hold no sway for you. You are prepared to overcome any barriers that you have built around you and you experience a fire in your heart that melts your harder emotions and softens you into feeling a warm, deep love. If, for example, you have previously been very rigid about your beliefs, you will now question these at a fundamental level. You will find yourself becoming much more tolerant of others as your heart opens. Perhaps, if you have held limiting attitudes towards money or sex, you may find yourself spending liberally on the things that bring you happiness or surrendering your body to new experiences of pleasure.

If you can both understand the true purpose of your soul mate connection and honour your union as a rich training ground in which you have volunteered to learn and help one another, you will be able to maintain this relationship for the length of your earthly lives to-gether. In other cases, you will find you are unable to sustain this high level of intensity over a long period. Often your contract together will be that you must part and that this parting will cause the final gift of soul searching and consequent self-revelation that you have to give to one another.

Soul mates can also be viewed in the light of a belief in reincarnation. It may be that you come together with your soul mate in this lifetime to clear the 'karma' that you both share. This 'karma' means that your souls have shared many lifetimes together and built up many emotional ties along the way. Over the aeons, you will have taken it in turns to teach each other soul lessons through various earth level hurts and awakenings. Now you may decide that you have learned enough together through hardship and want to elevate your connection to one of pure peace and harmony.

I have personally experienced this type of soul mate relationship. It caused me much passion, heart-opening and liberation, and it also gave me intense pain. Through this pain I was eventually able to reach, heal and expand parts of myself that I would never have accessed in any other way, because I was too frightened to face them in my customary reality. Only by taking a soul level approach of self-responsibility, forgiveness and real, all-encompassing love was I able to receive the enormous gifts that this relationship offered me. And this in turn has brought me to a place of karma-cleared peace with my soul mate.

So, if you are searching for or believe that you have found your soul mate, be prepared to take an advanced course in Spiritual Fitness and soul expansion! When you encounter your soul mate, begin with real gratitude in your heart. Then use your soul level thinking to guide you to some of the deepest, most challenging and most joyful experiences that you will ever have.

Being Single

Not all of our relationships are romantic and, in reality, they make up only a small percentage of our connections with others, (even though they seem to take up most of the space in our minds). Being single offers its own opportunities for self-exploration and expansion and is often an essential prelude to any kind of successful relationship. As we saw in the introduction to this course, all of life is cyclical and contains periods of action and assimilation. When you're not involved in a romantic relationship, it means that from a relationship angle, you are being given instead the opportunity to assimilate into your soul all that you have learned from previous partnerships.

If, for example, you feel that you have been overshadowed by your partners in the past, your time on your own offers you the opportunity to expand into your full personal power. Or, if you have been too controlling in past relationships, you will be given time to contemplate the price you have paid for this. You will be invited to consider letting down some of your self-defensive barriers and opening your heart to a more trusting and fluid connection with a partner.

Your primary relationship is always with yourself, regardless of whether or not you are in a romantic relationship. Throughout this WorkOut you will have noted that no relationship can be successful unless you approach it from the soul level perspective of self-responsibility, self-love and self-expansion. Before you can hope to achieve a fulfilling relationship with another, you'll need to be totally honest with yourself and accept responsibility for your own emotions, moods and attitudes. You will have to respect and be kind to yourself and avoid self-judgements that undermine you. And you will need to grant yourself the freedom to change, grow and shine.

If you find yourself craving a partner and seem unable to attract one, then remember that the same principles apply to getting a successful relationship as to keeping one. You are at your most attractive when you are in charge of your own emotions, when you radiate the inner peace that comes from self-love and when you make others feel respected and free to express who they truly are. Ultimately, all relationship issues come back to the fact that nobody can live your life for you. Nobody can feel your fear for you, experience your dark night of the soul or emerge with triumph, wisdom and humility into your true, divine self on your behalf. Nobody can learn your lessons for you or love you on your behalf. Certainly, others can love you and fill you with a wonderful sense of warmth and recognition, but only *you* can give yourself the validation you require to keep you balanced and whole within yourself. This way you will achieve the highest levels of Spiritual Fitness which are peace, joy and love. Then you will be able to compound these by sharing them with another soul on your mutual journeys of soul expansion. The feeling of connection that you seek to experience through your relationship with another starts through your connection with your own heart.

REVIEW

We seek out romantic relationships because we believe they will fulfil our basic human need for connection. This urge to connect reflects our longing to return to our natural and original state of joy, love, trust and hope.

Our adopted fears make us believe that we will be able to rediscover this state only through a romantic relationship with a partner. In fact, we first have to rediscover this state in our relationship with ourselves.

Our souls agree in advance with our partners which lessons we both need to learn together.

Self-love, respect and freedom are the essential components of a successful relationship. Our relationships are outer symbols of our inner worlds. Sex is one of the ways we express this inner reality. Our partners mirror for us the parts of ourselves that we need to look at.

A soul mate connection may not be a life partner connection and is a challenging and deeply life transforming experience. Being single gives you the chance to develop your most important relationship – the one with yourself.

THE INNER WORKOUT

I   Make a list of at least five qualities that you admire in your partner. Then write down at least five qualities that you dislike in them.

Be very honest with yourself and explore how many of the qualities you dislike in them. For example, do you find them impatient and quick-tempered, only to discover on closer inspection that, left to your own devices, you have an equally fiery nature of your own? Or do you think they're too slow and unimaginative when deep down you fear you may be that way too? Also, acknowledge these parts of yourself and treat them with compassion. Accept that they are simply unhealed parts of yourself that are based on previously unacknowledged fears. Allow yourself the freedom to change these fearful patterns by making a conscious effort to be aware of them and to overcome them whenever they occur.

As you come to terms with your own shortcomings and make peace with your weaker aspects, you will find yourself becoming far more tolerant of these in your partner. You may find that as you heal them in yourself and raise your own vibration, this will affect your partner and these qualities will also begin to disappear in them.

Spend the next week focusing on the qualities in your partner that you admire and on healing the negative qualities in yourself that they had previously been mirroring for you. After a week of this, you may well find that you want to make this approach a part of your daily life.

2 Imagine that it is your last day on Earth. Write a letter to your partner's soul from your soul. Honour who they are and the gifts that they have brought you and write down any heartfelt feelings that you may never have expressed.

You may then choose either to give them this letter or simply act upon it, by fully honouring them and expressing your true feelings towards them in the future.

3 Examine the external dramas in your life and see how they relate to your own inner struggle. If somebody at work is bullying you, how much does this reflect your own aggressive attitude to the more gentle part of yourself? If your partner belittles your intellectual abilities, how much does this echo your own opinion of your intelligence? Make a list of three of your most difficult relationships and write down the specific issues involved.

Next, instead of focusing on how to win in these external struggles, turn your attention inward and heal these struggles within yourself by systematically dismantling the fears behind them. For example, trust that you can be both powerful and gentle at the same time or find the courage inside you to express your intellectual side. This will help you to come to peace with those who have been enacting your dramas for you.

4 Act like you're in love! Just because you have become very familiar with someone does not mean that you should show them your most low key and casual self. Make the same effort with them that you would if you were meeting someone you admire for the first time. Dress up, sit up, have deep and interesting conversation with them. Remember how to flirt and dazzle them with the same charms you first used to attract them.

LEARNING
TO MEDITATE

**'Silence is the language God speaks and
everything else is a bad translation.'**

Father Thomas Keating

As you progress through this course, you may have noticed your focus turning increasingly inward. You may find the external events of your life seeming a little more distanced as you begin to understand them as the outer reflections of your inner world. In the last WorkOut we acknowledged your need to reconnect with your infinite self and saw the great importance of soul level thinking in achieving this. In this week's WorkOut you will be shown how to go completely inside yourself and connect directly with your highest, infinite self through meditation. This will strengthen your all-important capacity to think at a soul level until such thinking comes easily and naturally to you.

EXPLORING YOUR INNER WORLD

Many people spend the earlier part of their spiritual re-awakening looking outside themselves for their inner self. As we saw in WorkOut

Two, these people believe that if they adopt all the external trappings of spirituality they will somehow be able to gain enlightenment as if by osmosis. While all of these things have value in their own right, as you progress further along your spiritual path you'll find that all of the answers you seek live deep inside you. Therefore it becomes impossible for you to advance further along your path of spiritual re-awakening without knowing how to go inside yourself and tap into your inner wisdom. There is no substitute for this inner experience of the universal life force and the only way that you can truly access it is by disengaging from all external focus. You will then be able to enter into the heaven that you carry inside you.

This inner sanctuary is filled with purity and wonder. It is a place of peace and comfort, safety and warmth. To enter this world takes discipline since it requires the practice of meditation and silent contemplation.

The Power of Silence

When I take groups on retreat to the mountains of Sedona there are three key words that we use to encapsulate the experience. They are solitude, silence and sacredness. From observing these groups, I have learned that these three qualities are essential for us to gain any kind of understanding, transformation and inner peace in our lives. It is only when we are alone that we can truly get a clear sense of who we are, that we can delineate where we end and others begin. It is only in silence that we can hear the voice of the universal life force. And it is only in honouring the sacredness of our lives that we are able to experience the deep trust that is necessary to bring us peace.

Silence has become one of the rarest commodities of our modern day existence. Everywhere you turn you are bombarded with noise and external stimuli. Consequently, you spend most of your time responding to these outer signals and this leaves very little time and space to notice the signals that are coming from *inside* you. In this way, you soon start to lose sight of who you are. You get knocked off balance, find it hard to get in touch with your own real needs and instead you fulfil everyone else's. You may, for example, be in a job that demands that you deal with the public all day. Without time to enter into the silence inside your mind, you find that your focus is drawn entirely outside you. You then end up feeling 'strung out' and stressed as you concern yourself solely with the demands of those that you are talking to. Or are you part of a household that always has the TV or radio on in the background? Without being able to hear yourself think (quite liter-ally), you'll find your awareness is being completely directed by what-ever external information is being presented to you.

When you are able to enter into your own silence, you'll find that you reconnect with your infinite self. Beyond all your thoughts and emotions, deep down inside you there exists a centre of perfect peace. This is the part of you that is unaffected by the vicissitudes of your daily life because it is constantly linked to your source, to the universal life force of which you are a part. Like an invisible umbilical cord, this place of peace feeds you all your real power and sustenance. It is the part of you that actually gets you through life because it is the seat of your soul.

It is essential that you learn how to create this direct access to your soul since, energetically, it is your control centre. Rather than your life seeming to be made up of a random series of circumstances, your soul has actually set everything up to give you the best opportunities for growth. Your free will then decides which of these opportunities you accept and how quickly you do so. Without a deepened connection with your soul you may resist these invitations. You will then find that your life becomes erratic because you have chosen not to follow the path that was meant for your highest good. Therefore, connecting in silence with your soul allows you to make sense of and feel good about your life and helps to make it flow.

The Problem with Worrying

This soul connection also expands your awareness and stops you focusing on the petty aspects of your reality. Most people spend the majority of their time thinking negative thoughts and this is an exhausting waste of time and energy. If you'd like to check if you are one of these people, then try a short experiment right now. Stop for a moment and consider the kind of thinking that you've done in the last hour. How much of this time did you spend having fresh, original, peaceful thoughts and how much of your time was taken up with obsessive, repetitive worrying of some kind? If you're like most people, you will probably have found that the majority of your last hour's thinking was taken up with non-productive, earth level thinking.

This is the petty part of your mind that might make you wonder if you said the right thing to someone or ponder over what they said to you. Perhaps it will make you fret over how much money you have. Or it might keep you concerned about some future event, uncertain of how it will turn out and hoping it all goes according to plan. The problem with this type of thinking is that it will never bring you peace. As soon as you've come to some conclusion on one train of thought, along comes another, because earth level thinking is the level at which your mind really doesn't care what it thinks about, as long as it has something to play with. Like a dog with a bone it is recalcitrant and relentless and it needs to be constantly fed with problems.

To understand this better, let's take a look at the way your mind works. Whenever you have a thought about something, your mind automatically contracts around it. It's like passing over a map of the world and focusing in on a particular place. When you do this, you let go of your general awareness and narrow your field of vision. For most of us, this transforms into obsessive thinking. It is rare for us to have singular thoughts about anything. We pursue the same issue around our minds at least a handful of times no matter what it is and regardless of whether it's negative or positive.

Say, for example, you are thinking of the weekend that is approach-ing. Is one thought enough or do you have to make several turns around the subject? You might like to try this right now. First empty your mind and then cast your thoughts into the future and think about your forthcoming weekend for a moment ...

Were you actually able to have just one solo thought? Probably not! And this is what happens with just one (probably) innocuous topic. Now consider the process that you went through. Your mind was free and open, and then it suddenly contracted. When you become aware of this process you begin to understand the power that thought has, not only over your mind but also over your whole body. It also ex-plains how stressful thinking causes your body to constrict along with your mind and why you tense your muscles when you are under stress.

As we saw in WorkOut Two, most of your thinking is habitual. This means that you can retrain your mind to expand and to think habitu-ally with its big, infinite part. When you do this, you'll be able to silence the constant chatter and worrying of your earth level thinking and access the inner peace that comes from soul level thinking. Through the expanded awareness this gives you, you'll then begin to perceive the perfection in all things and understand the exquisite symmetry of the events in your life.

The Nature of the Inner Realms

As you go inside and enter the silence within you, your inner world becomes more 'real' and your external world starts to seem less real. You start to understand that there is no actual objective reality since your outer world is made up of neutral objects and events. These take on life only according to your subjective interpretations of them. For instance, are you the type of person that finds a fairground an exciting place to be, full of thrilling rides, or do you regard it as a frightening place since you don't find being terrified a pleasurable experience? Is there someone in your life who you really like who is profoundly disliked by someone else that you know? As the Talmud says, 'We do not see things as they are. We see them as we are.' Your external reality is actually made up of symbols that impress various feelings onto your soul.

Time and space are also different within your inner world. The events of your life are as big or as small as you let them be. For instance, if you look back over your day so far, there are certain incidents that will stand out and others that you have already forgotten. Those that stand out take up time and space in your mind which may be completely disproportionate to their actual occurrence in 'real' time. Perhaps you find yourself thinking of something embarrassing that you did. Even though this action may only have taken a moment or two, you may replay and magnify it in your mind until it seems to have taken much longer. This is because the length of time it takes up inside your reflective, inner world may be ten or even a hundred times greater than the duration of the actual event itself.

Within your inner world, time expands and contracts at your will because here you are operating at soul level awareness instead of the earth level, man-made one, and time is a man-made concept. When I lead groups in guided meditation, the participants frequently tell me that forty-five minutes' meditation seems more like fifteen. At other times, you may have noticed that if you're waiting for a bus that is late, fifteen minutes can seem more like forty-five! This discrepancy occurs because *subjectively* these two experiences are very different. In the former case, the group members are willingly exploring their subconscious states and connecting with their infinite, timeless selves. In the latter, the focus is on the man-made earth level world of time. When you enter into your inner realms you detach from finite earth level reality. Your consciousness expands into the infinite universe where eternity is one moment that lasts forever. In infinity time has no meaning.

Knowing versus Thinking

When you become more adept at connecting with your infinite self, you will start to benefit from your soul's deep wisdom. As we have seen throughout this course, soul level thinking gives you a much more enlightened perspective on the events of your life. It will, for example, give you the outlook that there are no bad things that happen, only good things that take longer to understand. And, as you connect more and more with your innate wisdom, you'll find yourself moving away from making judgments. Instead you will make observations based on your inner knowing. Then you can use your discretion to avoid anything that feels inappropriate to your highest purpose.

When you start to experience this 'knowing' of your soul's awareness, you are moving from logical, left brain thinking to intuitive, right brain feeling. Within the inner realms of your consciousness, your intuition is paramount. Without having to analyse situations, you will just 'know' what they are all about. Instead of reacting to the façade that people and situations present to you, you will feel the motives and the messages behind them. When you go inside and replay conversations you had or events that took place, they will echo around your mind and with each ricochet, their true meaning will become more apparent. You will then discover that your mind is starting to operate simultaneously in several dimensions. You'll be able to access the material, emotional, mental and spiritual aspects of each situation to give you a much fuller understanding.

As you become more connected with your inner worlds, you will also move beyond your limiting beliefs because your underlying attitude will be based on pure love and faith. We shall explore this attitude in depth in the remaining two WorkOuts but first let's take a look at how you can enter the silence inside you and access these inner realms.

HOW TO MEDITATE EFFECTIVELY

Meditation is a confusing and sometimes threatening word for many people. For some reason, we have been taught that there are set ways for us to meditate, (or talk to the universal life force), as if this were simply a standard, universal pursuit with no personal input. When people come to me and tell me that they're unable to meditate, I always reply as follows. Imagine that someone is trying to tell you that there is only one joke in the world and that you must find it funny and laugh at it. If you don't happen to find it amusing, they will tell you, and you will be convinced, that you don't have a sense of humour. Yet the fact is that some people like slapstick, some like trenchant wit and some like practical jokes – we can all find something that makes us laugh but we do not all laugh at the same things. Similarly, if I were to tell you that there is only one way to meditate, (such as cross-legged and upside down while chanting 'om'), you would also be convinced that you are unable to do so.

Meditation is the way that we connect with our divine source and essence. As such it is a highly personal and individual experience and it is *not exactly alike for any two people.* Just like making love or finding what makes you laugh, it is an expression of your deepest essence and has subtleties that make it entirely unique to you.

Finding the Right Style of Meditation for You

Since meditation is another way of using your internal faculties, before you can begin to meditate successfully you need to know how these faculties work best for you. The way that you meditate usually mirrors the way that you think. Your thought processes can be broken down into what are known as three basic representational systems – visual, auditory or kinesthetic. This means that you think with your senses, and see, hear or feel all your experiences, (with some smell and taste thrown in along the way). Sometimes you will use only one representational system (or sense) and sometimes a combination. For example, stop and think for a moment of whatever you were doing before you picked up this book …

You'll find that either you made pictures of that time in your mind (visual), and/or you talked to yourself about it in your mind (auditory) and/or you experienced the feelings you felt at the time (kinesthetic). With meditation, you'll probably find that the method that suits you best is based on the same type, or combination, of representational systems that you have just used to think.

When I first began on my path of spiritual re-awakening, I remember my friends trying to get me to meditate in an attempt to alleviate the considerable chaos that was characteristic of my life at the time. I re- call speaking on the phone to one friend in particular and telling her how sad, unhappy and out of control I was feeling. In response, she suggested that I imagine myself surrounded by a bubble of white light, which she assured me would protect me from the negativity I was experiencing in my outer world. Since 'visual' is my least developed representational system, I had great difficulty in getting myself to pic- ture any such thing. I strained and strained, like a blocked artist trying to magic a reluctant image out of thin air, and all the while the calm, focused state I was trying to achieve was being eroded by my feelings of ineptitude and inadequacy. When I eventually did get an image, it seemed totally contrived and it didn't help make me feel any better. I later ran into several other 'visual' people who attempted to lead me through the kind of guided meditations that involved either seeing colours or visualizing myself in a certain place in minute detail. Again, it proved too difficult and before long I had dismissed meditation as something that I couldn't do and something that didn't work.

Shortly after this, I was introduced to Transcendental Meditation as a means of managing stress. This worked much better for me because it was based on an auditory representational system that involved the silent inner repetition of a mantra. Since one of my main ways of perceiving reality is through hearing, the introduction of a recurring sacred sound into my mind had a powerfully hypnotic effect on me and enabled me to withdraw into my inner world. This kept me going for a while but I discovered that I could only go so far with this process before I became distracted. Clearly there was a vital element still missing in my quest for a meditation style that worked for me.

Some time later, I came across various Buddhist meditations that involved focusing on the breath as the primary way to connect with one's soul. This proved to be the most powerful and effective method for me since my strongest representational system is kinesthetic (with auditory a close second). When I was taught to put feeling and hearing together by silently counting my breath to myself during meditation, I finally discovered the exact way of meditating that worked for me. Later in this WorkOut I shall discuss this and other methods of meditating in depth. Before that, let's look at how you can set up your surroundings in the way that is most conducive to meditation for you.

Creating a Sacred Environment

Since meditation is the way that you connect with your soul, which is the most sacred part of you, then the best way to prepare for your meditation is by creating a sacred place for it in your life. For example, it is pointless trying to connect with your inner world if your outer world is liable to intrude at any moment. So you need to find a place where you will not be disturbed, which means avoiding phones and making sure that you are left completely alone (including by pets). Again, the more seriously that you treat your meditation, the more seriously those around you will treat it too.

Use your awareness of your representational systems to help create the perfect setting. If you are very visual, then you will respond well to an area that is filled with beautiful sacred objects, candles and fabrics in your favourite colours. You might like to surround this area with pictures of places in nature that particularly inspire you or of animals with which you feel a strong spiritual connection. If you are primarily auditory, you might like to play gentle, hypnotic music in the background, or a recording of the sound of waves on the shore, or listen to the constant flow of a fountain. And, if you are especially kinesthetic (which means tactile as well as emotionally feeling), you might like to fill your sacred place with lots of luxurious cushions and burn incense to transport you into loftier realms.

When you have done this, notice the flow of energy in the room or area, remove any unnecessary items and keep this space clean and clear. Next, you can work with your own energy to make sure that when you meditate you are facing the direction that feels best for you and that the whole area is set up to flow with your particular sense of balance and peace. This place is your sanctuary and the portal through which you cross from one world to another. The most important thing about setting up your meditation space is that it feels sacred, relaxing and uplifting to you.

Starting to Meditate

Many people are put off at an early stage in their introduction to meditation because they are told that there are set ways to do it. For example, a woman came to me and told me that she was unable to meditate because her partner, who was a yoga devotee, insisted that she sit in a certain way with her hands in a certain position before she could begin. Since she was not a yoga practitioner herself, this posture was very uncomfortable for her and too much of a distraction from any kind of inner peace. I told her to go and meditate in a separate room and sit whichever way felt most natural to her. Some people like to sit up when they meditate and others prefer to lie down. Generally, I have found that sitting up is best because it helps you feel your connection between heaven and earth and also encourages you to stay awake! The only thing that I strongly recommend is that you keep your spine straight, so that your energy fields can align themselves most powerfully.

So, with your ambience set up and your body in the posture that is best suited to bring you to stillness, you are ready to begin your meditation. To do so you first need to connect with your own internal rhythm. Just as you have a pulse, a heartbeat and a breathing rhythm, so you have a unique inner beat that is your own metronome. When you follow the gentle oscillation of this rhythm, it has a hypnotic effect on you and starts to lull you into a sense of relaxation and deep peace. (As you get more proficient at this, you will also begin to notice the different rhythms of everyone and everything around you. You'll then be able to detach from any that don't resonate with your own and constantly return to your own rhythm to keep yourself balanced.)

I have found that the best way to connect with my inner metronome is with my eyes shut, because doing so makes me use my inner sight. It also makes my hearing and feeling senses stronger. Again, I must emphasize that there are no specific rules to meditating so you must do whatever works best for you. If you choose to keep your eyes open then it's best to keep them focused on one spot so that your visual sense is not distracting you.

Next, bring your awareness into your physical body, just breathe normally and start to pull your awareness back inside yourself. The whole purpose of this exercise is that you begin to delineate the difference between your outer and inner worlds. You start to detach your energy from the world around you and move your focus to your self and your essence. You can begin this process by feeling the weight of your body being supported by the ground beneath you and noticing how fast or how slow your inner movement feels. If you've had a hectic few hours, you may well feel as if your energy is scattered or spinning and this will keep your mind racing and make it difficult for you to move into meditation. To remedy this you can choose one of several options.

The first is to slow yourself down by taking long, deep breaths. Another, completely different approach, is to breathe in such a gentle way that if you imagined a feather in front of your face, it would not be disturbed by your breath. A more abstract way is to imagine that you can feel the heartbeat of the earth beneath you and allow its gravitational pull to connect you with your own strong, silent and steady rhythm. Whichever you choose, begin to focus solely on the rise and the fall of your own breath and you will find that this has a gradual, hypnotic and relaxing effect on you, in much the same way as a mother gently rocks her baby to sleep with slow, undulating movements.

Once you have connected with your own rhythm and have succeeded in detaching your physical awareness from the outside world, you can begin to direct your inner awareness away from your thoughts and into your feelings. This usually takes practice and it involves constantly shifting your awareness back to the blank backdrop behind your thoughts, instead of trying to banish them. (There are more exercises to help you move beyond your thoughts at the end of this WorkOut.) As you follow this process you will enter into an altered state of consciousness and will be able to expand your awareness into a far deeper understanding of your life and the universe in which you live.

MEDITATION TECHNIQUES

The father of modern hypnosis, Milton Erickson, described the trance state as the 'loss of the multi-foci of attention'. By this he meant that when we meditate we narrow our range of inner focus until we still our minds and concentrate on just one thing. To experience this for yourself, you might like to try a little experiment right now. Look around the area you are in and take in as much visual information as possible. Now with your hand, form the 'ok' sign, that is, make a circle with the tips of your thumb and forefinger touching. Close one eye and hold the circle up close to your open eye and look around this area again through the circle. You will find that the details you are looking at seem more magnified. In reality they are not but, because you are isolating each detail and giving it your full, undivided attention, it seems a lot clearer to you. This is the same effect that meditation produces inside us as we contemplate our inner world. Everything becomes more lucid and understandable to us because we have eliminated all extraneous thoughts.

To enter into this meditative state, here is a selection of methods you can choose from. Using one or more of these, everyone who has come to me to learn meditation has been able to achieve at the very least a deeply relaxed state and at best complete fusion with their soul. The most important thing to remember is that you meditate not with your mind but with your heart. For meditation to be effective, I have found that ten minutes is the minimum time you will need. Start small and work up to as long a time as you can. I have also found that morning is the best time to meditate because it sets us up for our day.

You will definitely get the most benefit from the following section if you try out each method as you read about it. Since we have already begun with your breath and since breathing is universal, let's look first at some breathing techniques that you can use to take you into a deep meditative state. I'll start with some of the more straightforward ones and move onto the more abstract.

Breathing Techniques

I COUNTING YOUR BREATH

As you breathe in and out, grouping each inhalation and exhalation together as one breath, silently count your breaths up to the number ten. When you get there, keep going but this time count your breaths back down to the number one. Again, when you reach number one, start the process all over again. Eventually you may notice the counting slip away as you connect with your own internal rhythm. The most important thing is that you remain unconcerned about whether or not you are still counting and focus only on the rise and fall of your breath, like the infinite ebb and flow of the tide. A woman who came to me saying she was unable to meditate found this technique so effective that, a few months later, she was able to use it to significantly lower her blood pressure before surgery.

2 SPACED BREATHING

This technique involves taking as much time as possible between your breaths. It is in the spaces between your breaths that your infinite self lives. This is why when someone sneezes we bless them, because sneezing involves entering the space where we disconnect from our human lifeline of oxygen for just a second. To use this technique, breathe gently and slowly and count to five for each inhalation, hold your breath for the count of five, and then exhale to the count of five.

3 BREATHING WITH THE UNIVERSE

This is a more abstract but equally powerful technique. To use it effectively, first you will need to take your awareness out into the universe. Feel the infinity that surrounds you and then imagine this living organism breathing in and out. Synchronize your breathing with the breath of the universe until you feel at one with all things. By expanding your energy first out and then inwards in this way, you heighten your awareness of the other dimensions of reality that we live in. Whenever I have used this method with groups in guided meditation, they have reported feeling totally transported into altered states of consciousness.

Meditating with Sound

A good way to enhance the hypnotic effect of your breathing is by accompanying it with the introduction of sound. Since, at the vibrational level, you are made up of light and sound, when you open yourself up to the sound vibrations around you you automatically change your state of consciousness. Because of the bio-chemical effect that words have on your entire system, the use of mantras, (which are repeated sounds or phrases), is a powerful transformational technique. Let's look now at how language and sound can be used to guide your awareness into your inner realms.

I MANTRAS

If you synchronize your breathing with the silent repetition of a sound, word or phrase, you'll find that your inner rhythm grows stronger. For example, as we saw in WorkOut Three, you can silently say the phrase 'I am' on your in breath and then silently say the word 'peace' on your out breath. Other words such as 'purity', 'love' or 'strength' are also good to follow 'I am'. As you inhale with each 'I am', imagine that you are pulling in from the universe the quality that follows, such as 'peace'. When you breathe out, feel the quality flooding through your whole being. If you repeat this mantra for several moments you'll find your awareness becoming focused at the centre of your being. It will help you to feel still and grounded.

In Transcendental Meditation you are given a Sanskrit word as your mantra, which is repeated silently throughout your meditation. This method is based on the belief that while your mind is occupied with the mantra, your natural state of peace and joy can rise to the surface. It is a powerful tool if used consistently and can even produce physical levitation, as witnessed in some of the more advanced practitioners of Transcendental Meditation.

2 CHANTING

Most religions use some form of chant or incantation to induce a sense of the sacred. Perhaps the best known of these is the Sanskrit mantra 'om', (or 'aum'), which has now become widely familiar in Western culture. In the West the use of spoken or sung Latin has been used for hundreds of years as a kind of holy language to inspire instant reverence.

When you chant a word or sound out loud, it vibrates throughout your whole body and energy field. If you find the word or sound that is right for you, it will raise your own vibration to a higher frequency.

Personally, I find that the use of words that have no literal meaning to me, such as 'om', are most powerful for this purpose because when I chant them, I can't be distracted by their meaning. Consequently, I relate only to their resonance inside me.

In the next section you will be given such sounds for each of your chakras and these are extremely powerful tools to help you access an altered state of consciousness.

3 SINGING BOWLS

If you prefer to move away from words and syllables to pure sound, you may like to try meditating to the sound of 'singing' bowls. Tibetan singing bowls have now become quite familiar in the West and are traditionally made of a unique alloy of seven precious metals. Each bowl has its own special sound. To produce this sound, the bowl is rubbed or struck with a wooden stick, (known as a *puja*), which produces overtones that are soothing and uplifting. They have been used in the East for thousands of years to invoke trance states.

Alternatively, crystal singing bowls are made from quartz crystal and when rubbed with a stick produce a harmonic tone. Different bowls give off different notes and it is possible to get one for each of the seven major notes from C to B, which correspond to each of the seven chakras. Again the purity of sound from these bowls and the high frequency it emits are very good for inducing altered states of awareness.

Certain types of bells can also be used for a similar effect to that of singing bowls.

4 DRUMS

I have been fortunate enough to make my own Native American drum, a flat, circular hand-held drum with an open back, and sometimes I will beat this drum in rhythm with my breath or heartbeat to send myself into a deep meditative state. Drumbeats can be both grounding and liberating since you can feel their very physical vibrations throughout your body and soul. There are many images of tribal peoples of all cultures dancing themselves into a trance state to the sound of the drum and, at a more advanced level, it is possible to go on what is known as 'shamanic journeying' solely by being transported by the powerful beat of the drum. In the earlier stages, all you need is a gentle drumbeat to connect to your own inner metronome.

5 TAPES

Many people listen to meditation tapes when they first start meditating. There are lots on the market and, as with everything else, you need to find the ones that work best for you. I can personally recommend any by Denise Linn, Louise Hay or, of course, myself! You can also listen to tapes of music or sounds of nature to help you to move into a relaxed state. As you become more used to meditating, you will most likely find that you no longer need to use tapes, but as a starting point they can be very helpful.

Meditating with Visualization

Those of you who are primarily visual probably have the greatest scope for different meditation techniques because, when you take your awareness inside, you can conjure up any images that you like. Here are some of the more common visual methods.

1 PICTURING A SACRED PLACE

There is special place for each of us, whether real or imaginary, whether we have been there or not, that makes us feel most connected to the universal life force. For some, it is a mountain landscape, where the earth touches the sky, for others an ocean scene or, perhaps, an image of a forest. The beauty and power you perceive in your special place reflect the beauty and power inside you so that, when you contemplate this scene, it instantly transports you into a higher state of consciousness. To achieve this state, you need either to focus on a photo of such a place when you meditate or simply conjure it up in your mind's eye. The more clearly you can imagine yourself *inside* this image, with bright colours and clear, lifesize outlines, the more powerful and effective it will become as you merge with its inner essence. Sometimes you can focus on and be inspired by an image of a living creature, such as an eagle, dolphin or wolf, with the same results.

2 FOCUSING ON AN EXTERNAL OBJECT

If you prefer to keep your eyes open during meditation, you can focus your vision on a single object such as a candle flame or a flower petal. The concentration that you use to focus on your outer world in this way will be mirrored in your inner world and will bring your mind to stillness. For this process it's usually best to lower your eyelids slightly. Some Indian spiritual masters, who are well versed in the art of meditation, recommend that we should meditate with our eyes slightly open as this prevents us from falling asleep. Personally, I don't find this necessary but again you must simply do what feels right for you.

3 SACRED SYMBOLS

There are certain symbols and shapes that are regarded as sacred. These have been used for thousands of years by many cultures to represent aspects of alternate realities. For example, the spiral appears in Australian Aboriginal, Native American and Celtic sacred imagery, to name but a few. Hindu and Buddhist practices use mandalas, which are usually elaborate circular designs symbolizing the universe. If you focus intently on these images, either externally or in your mind, their sacred essence can help you to connect with your deep, subconscious awareness. Sometimes, as you become more proficient in your meditation, certain shapes and symbols will appear in your mind's eye. While some have a widely accepted universal meaning, I believe it is their personal relevance to you that is most important in your deciphering of them.

4 COLOUR AND LIGHT

Many members of my meditation groups say that they see a variety of vivid colours when they enter into a meditative state. These colours have the effect of further expanding their inner awareness. If you can deliberately summon up colours or different shades of light inside your mind, you should be able to achieve similar results and this method is at the root of many creative visualization techniques. You may like to begin either by imagining yourself surrounded by a particular colour or by visualizing it running through you.

Another powerful use of colour comes through an awareness of your chakra system. Since colour is only one property of the chakras, let's take a closer look at what they are.

The Chakras

Much has been talked and written about chakras and you will often find that interpretations differ slightly from one another but there are general qualities that recur throughout. Ultimately, since your chakras are part of your unique soul's make-up, it is your personal interpretation of them that is most valid and real for you. Focusing on your chakras during meditation helps you connect with your own inner consciousness and is also a highly effective way to sense any imbalances in your being.

Just as your body has physical energy centres such as your heart, lungs and brain, you also have a subtle, outer body known as your aura or your etheric body. This body has seven main energy centres or chakras. *Chakra* is a Sanskrit word meaning 'wheel of light'. To those who can see or sense them, chakras are perceived as spinning discs whose energy extends through your physical body and out into the universe. Certain emotional, spiritual and physical characteristics are attributed to each of your chakras and each has a colour and a sound of its own. I also think of chakras as power engines that supply us with different types or qualities of energy.

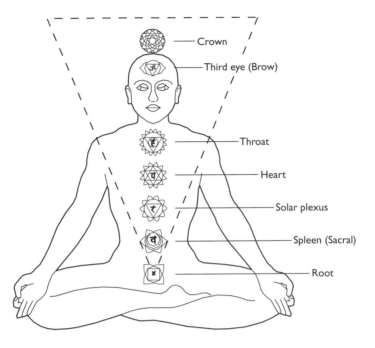

I perceive the characteristics of chakras as being symbolized by an upside down pyramid – as shown above. The narrowest point at the bottom of this pyramid is your root chakra, which is where your awareness is at its most narrow and self-centred. As you move up through your chakras, your awareness expands outwards until at the widest point at the top of the pyramid, where your crown chakra is situated, you are connected to the universal consciousness. Opening your chakras is a very powerful meditative tool and so that you can use them most effectively, let's take a look at what each one of them represents.

First Chakra – Name *Root* – Colour *Red* – Sound *Lam* – Engine *Physical*
Situated at the base of your spine, this chakra rules your physical life force and vitality. It deals with primal issues of physical survival such as money, food and domestic security. It affects your lower intestines,

legs and feet and skeletal structure. The root chakra is where you are entirely caught up in self-absorption. It connects you to the world through your physical body.

Second Chakra – Name *Spleen* or *Sacral* – Colour *Orange* – Sound *Vam* – Engine *Emotional*

Situated four finger-widths below your navel, this chakra rules your desires, emotions, passion, sexual energy, sensuality and creativity. It is sometimes referred to as the 'lower heart' in women and it governs the emotional aspects of your relationships. It affects your reproductive organs, pelvis, kidneys and bladder. In the spleen chakra you are aware of others but are relating to them at very much an earth level that involves trying to get your most basic emotional and sexual needs met. It connects you to the world through your emotional awareness.

Third Chakra – Name *Solar Plexus* – Colour *Yellow* – Sound *Ram* – Engine *Willpower*

Situated between your navel and the bottom of your ribcage, this chakra rules your personal power, self-awareness, self-esteem, authority, judgment and willpower. It governs how you seek to control the world around you and live your purpose. It affects your digestive system, liver, lower back, gall bladder and nervous system. In the solar plexus chakra your awareness expands and you realize that you can get what you want by using your mind and willpower. It connects you to the world through your personal power.

Fourth Chakra – Name *Heart* – Colour *Green* – Sound *Yam* – Engine *Love*

Situated at the centre of your breastbone, this chakra rules your love, compassion, forgiveness, self-acceptance, healing, innocence and joy. It regenerates your body and psyche. It affects your heart, lungs, chest, upper back, circulatory system and skin. In the heart chakra you open up to the power of love as a way to connect with others. It connects you to the world through love.

Fifth Chakra – Name *Throat* – Colour *Blue* – Sound *Ham* – Engine Communication

Situated at the base of your throat, this chakra rules your communication, trust, self-expression, and confidence. It is where you express your creativity and it deals with everything related to sound and the voicing of truth and your authentic self. It affects your throat, vocal chords, glands, mouth and speech. In the throat chakra, you start to refine your communication with others into self-expression and trust. It connects you to the world through your communicative voice.

Sixth Chakra – Name *Third Eye or Brow* – Colour *Indigo* – Sound *Ksham* – Engine *Intuition*

Situated between your eyebrows, this chakra rules your intuition, psychic ability, freethinking, mental balance and visualization. It is where you develop clairvoyance. It affects your vision, sinuses, pituitary gland and ears. In the third eye chakra your awareness expands even more and you connect with others through pure inner knowing. It connects you to the world through your intuitive faculty.

Seventh Chakra – Name *Crown* – Colour *Violet, White or Gold* – Sound *Om* – Engine *Spiritual*

Situated at the top and centre of your head, this chakra rules your spirituality, universal consciousness, faith and purity. It strengthens your immune system and is the portal through which you access divine energy. It affects your brain, nervous and muscular systems and skull. In the crown chakra you experience complete oneness with the universal life force and connect directly with the souls of those around you. It connects you to the world through spiritual awareness.

Once you have found a meditative style that works for you, you can use any or all of your representational systems to open your chakras – that is, you can see, hear or feel them opening and closing. Then, imagine these discs of light spinning in front of, through, and behind you, and use your *feelings* to ascertain which need strengthening and balancing. To strengthen them, picture, hear or feel each one of them expanding and then all of them aligning at the same level of intensity. This is an excellent way for you to do a regular health check on your energy and to enhance your Spiritual Fitness. When you have finished meditating with your chakras, always close them and send them inside again like flower petals closing up at night.

In the Inner WorkOut exercises that follow, you'll find several meditations that will help you to expand your consciousness and form a strong, clear bond with your soul and with the universal life force. As with everything else, meditation gets better with practice and this takes discipline. The good news is that, despite all our resistance, I have never yet met anyone who didn't feel better after they had meditated. As you meditate more and more, the benefits of calmness, love, understanding and focused energy will inspire you to keep on developing this sacred connection with your soul.

REVIEW

As you progress along your spiritual path, you will have to go deeper inside yourself to gain the power of spiritual connection. To enter into the silence within you and connect with your soul and the universal life force, you need to meditate.

The more that you enter into your inner realms, the more you realize that your inner world is the one that is most real for you and that your external world is merely symbolic. As you become more connected with your inner world you will be able to transcend the false limiting beliefs of your outer, imagined real world.

To still your mind to meditate you first need to move away from negative thoughts and free up space in your mind for your soul to speak to you. To do this it helps to create a sacred space in which to meditate.

Meditation is a highly personal experience and uses your senses of seeing, hearing and feeling in whichever combination is most effective for you. Try different techniques until you find one that works for you.

Your chakras will give you a good insight into your overall state of well-being.

Meditation will bring you peace, focus, love, joy and understanding.

THE INNER WORKOUT

Before you begin these exercises, you will need to have found out which meditation style works best for you. If you don't have any bowls, bells or drums to hand you can skip trying those for the moment. You can always give them a go when the opportunity arises!

1   If you already have a meditation space in your home, you might like to check that it reflects your most dominant representational system(s). Create a space for yourself that will make you want to be in it and will encourage you to meditate.

2   You can *always* find time to meditate. Fifteen minutes first thing in the morning will set you up in a much calmer and more focused state for the rest of the day and this will allow you to be much more economical with your time and energy throughout your day.

3   When you first begin to meditate you may find that uncalled-for thoughts intrude and distract you. To remedy this, you can try whichever of the following techniques is most natural for you.

Visual Techniques – Picture your thoughts in a bubble and watch them drift off into the distance.

Auditory Techniques – Either use a mantra to 'drown out' the noise of your thinking or instead, turn down the volume of your thoughts.

Kinesthetic Techniques – Imagine your thoughts going off to think for themselves while you drop your awareness below them and your conscious mind and feel with your heart instead.

Meditation is an organic process and so it will be different each time. Some days you'll find it easy and on others it may take you 15 minutes or so just to settle your mind. You may take heart from the fact that even the most experienced meditators have days when they find it hard to concentrate, so just be still, persist with your techniques and eventually you will shift into an altered state of consciousness.

4   If there are any distracting external noises that you cannot control, take your awareness to the infinite silence that is behind them. As you do so you'll gradually find your consciousness merging with this silent, infinite backdrop and it will calm your mind and expand your soul. You can also use this technique to move your focus away from your thoughts and into the vast, empty canvas on which they appear.

5   Now that you have discovered which methods of meditation work best for you, you can use your meditation to explore your inner worlds.

A basic opening technique for this is to take your focus inside you and imagine yourself at the top of a wide staircase. Imagine that this staircase has ten steps and, as you allow yourself to descend it, you will find your awareness dropping deeper and deeper into its subconscious state. With each step, slow yourself down and become more aware of the space between your breaths. Remember a time when you felt completely at peace, then allow this feeling to flood through your being. When you reach the bottom, imagine stepping off this staircase and into the infinite universe you carry inside you. Try to stay in this place for at least ten minutes. When it is time for you to return to normal, waking consciousness, count yourself up to ten, take in some deep breaths, stretch your body and gently open your eyes.

6   Allow yourself to go into a meditative state and place your hand on whichever part of your body you feel is the centre of your soul's consciousness, such as your heart, solar plexus or third eye. Next, slowly connect with your own inner rhythm, imagine its beat and movement, and when you feel fully at one with it, move your hand in a gentle motion that feels like the dance of this rhythm. This helps you to solidify your connection with your soul's energy.

TAKING THE LEAP & FINDING YOUR PURPOSE

**'You either kiss the future
or the past goodbye.'**

Ringo Starr

Congratulations on making it this far! Your journey through this course has taken you deeper and deeper inside yourself on a voyage of self-discovery. Now it's time to move outwards again and explore the way your inner transformation will manifest in your outer world. As the practice of regular meditation strengthens your connection with your soul, you'll begin to feel the rumblings of your true self emerging into your everyday life. If you are not prepared for this, it may at first seem a strange and unnerving experience.

In this week's WorkOut we will look at the ways in which you can make the transition from your old world into your new life as smooth as possible. We shall also explore how you can prepare yourself to step into your greatness and find your purpose in this lifetime.

THE TRANSITION PERIOD

The process of spiritual re-awakening has a built-in transition period through which everyone must pass. In the infinite wisdom of the universal intelligence, this has been designed to protect you. During your time of re-awakening, you may feel as if you have one foot in your old world and one in your new. This crossover period is set up to help you to cope with the significant changes you are experiencing.

Later in this WorkOut we'll look at the new resources you can find within you as part of your transformed self. First, let's look at some of the obstacles you may encounter during this period of transition and discover what they mean.

Spiritual Adolescence

As you learn more about yourself and understand the world from a new and deeper perspective, you'll find yourself moving away from certain aspects of your past. These may begin to seem restrictive and uninteresting to you in much the same way that we all feel about our childhood when we reach adolescence. This is the time when you experience your spiritual adolescence. It is when you are caught between your childlike desire for the security that you have known, (with its lesser responsibilities), and the autonomy of a more mature belief system. For instance, at this stage you may wish you could work for yourself, using your own creative skills, but at the same time do not feel prepared to give up the security of a steady income. Just as with adolescence, this is a 'rite of passage'.

During this period you may find yourself making awkward attempts to fuse your past and future as you struggle with your true identity. For instance, you might take crystals into the office, much to the derision of your co-workers while, at the other end of the spectrum, still feeling unable to do without your mobile phone on a retreat! During this time of spiritual adolescence, you may also feel too big and expanded for your old life but not yet ready to live a life totally based on Spiritual Fitness. For example, endless nights of carousing may now seem pretty meaningless to you and yet the thought of sitting down and expressing your vulnerability to one of your peers may still fill you with anxiety. Or you may be bored with your old routine and want to spread your wings and fly, yet still be afraid to travel alone or venture out to new places to make new friends.

This is also a time of experimentation. There are many spiritual schools of thought out there and some will be right for you and some won't. In approaching these you can use your growing intuition to guide you but it is probably wise to avoid any that are based on a cult of personality. The path of spiritual re-awakening is about *self*-discovery and *self*-empowerment and, ultimately, this means that *you* are your greatest spiritual teacher since *you* are the world expert on yourself. Other people can certainly give you the benefit of their experience and wisdom, but only you can connect with your own soul and your creator. You don't need a third party to do this for you.

In all cases, it is very important that you travel strictly at your own pace. This means you shouldn't compare your progress with anyone's but your own. For instance, if someone you know has just received their twenty-fifth healing certificate and someone else has been reliving a past life canoeing up the Amazon, this really has no relevance for your own soul's journey! Just look at your own life and see how far you have already come in the past months. I often notice a kind of competitiveness in the way people interact during their spiritual re-awakening. This stems from a feeling that they should be going faster, and this makes them try to stay on a par with the activities of those around them. This is an earth level response to a soul level issue. We each have our own unique rhythm and our own personal rate of evolution best suited for our learning. If you find yourself constantly comparing your development with that of others, remember that to compete with another is to detract from your own energy field. To compete with yourself is to revitalize it. Spiritual Fitness is about having authentic power and that means doing what feels right for *you* and doing it in *your own time*.

Another interesting aspect of this period is that normally you will not be able to access your full power until you are responsible enough to handle it. By way of illustration, most children in this world can reach the pedals of a car by the age of eleven. This means that with a little training they would soon be able to drive. Yet our laws don't allow them out onto our roads until several years later because they have not yet built up enough awareness to be safe to themselves and others. So it is with us. As the saying goes, 'A little knowledge is a dangerous thing', and until you are able fully to grasp the concepts of Spiritual Fitness and *live* them you will be protected from using them inappropriately. So, if you feel that things aren't moving quickly enough and you're feeling frustrated because you still can't see auras or find your purpose in life, just be patient – it will all come to you when you are ready.

During this transition period you may also feel the need to share with others your 'youthful' enthusiasm about the positive changes that you have already noticed in your life. Remember that you are still at a very tender stage in your spiritual re-awakening, so it's best to share your excitement only with people who are sympathetic to such notions and who understand what you are going through. If you try to communicate your experiences to those who don't know what you're talking about, their negativity may undo some of the good work that you have already achieved. Their fear-based cynicism may cause you to doubt yourself as it latches onto the remaining vestiges of fear that you still have inside you. Until you reach spiritual maturity and are able to stand in your own power and not be swayed by those around you, choose your company wisely and share your experiences only with those who will treat them with respect.

The Inevitability of Change

As we saw in WorkOut Two, if you are involved in a process of spiritual transformation then, by definition, you are going to have to experience changes in your life. The soul searching that you've been doing may be beginning to provide you with the very answers you have been searching for. The only problem is that they may not at first seem like the answers you want! As you connect with your soul and your highest purpose, you may be surprised to find that some of the key areas of your life need a total overhaul since they have been based on your old inauthentic self.

I often come across this in my Spiritual Fitness WorkOut Groups. People start to feel that they are in the wrong job or relationship and then begin to experience great dissatisfaction with their lives. If this should happen to you, there are two very important points that you should bear in mind. The first is that the dissatisfaction you are feeling may seem new but it is, in fact, an old, buried emotion emerging from a place deep inside you. The second is that it's unwise to make any sudden, dramatic decisions based on this emotion until you have understood exactly what fears are at the base of it. Otherwise, you risk starting up a new life but recreating your dissatisfaction in a new environment.

At this point, you may wonder, 'How will I know when it's the right time for me to take action and make the changes that my new outlook is leading me to?' The answer to this is simply, 'You'll know because you won't have any choice.' There will be no decision to make because it will become unbearable for you to remain a moment longer in any situation that doesn't serve your highest good and reflect your truth. Nor will you have to make this decision single-handedly. When the time is right for you to make your move, you will be helped along by the universal intelligence that wants to see you happy, in your truth and totally fulfilled.

One of my own major life changes was a perfect example of this principle. As I have previously mentioned, I had been working in nightclubs for a very long period. In the later years I had also been running workshops in my spare time and I was moving gradually along my path of spiritual re-awakening. Eventually, my health took a turn for the worse and I decided I needed to take a sabbatical for nine months. I spent this time in my spiritual home of Sedona, where I enjoyed a blissful time connecting with my soul and clearing out a lot of my old fearful patterns.

When I returned to my job after this symbolic nine-month period of gestation, I felt as if my spiritual self had been totally reborn. I tried my best to fit back into my job but where, previously, my spirituality had been a sideline and a source of entertainment for my co-workers, I soon realized that it had now become the main focus of my being. I found myself getting more and more distracted in my job and within a year was consistently making the kind of mistakes that happen when your mind is elsewhere. I was still not ready to go out into the world and make a living from my workshops and counselling – in fact, the thought quite terrified me. Yet, when the time is right, we are all forced to fly the nest whether we feel we are ready or not and that is what happened to me.

A short time later, my soul mate was undergoing surgery in the US and I felt a very strong urge to be there. In the past, my length of service at the nightclub had always allowed me to take time off whenever I chose, but on this occasion I was astounded when my boss told me that I couldn't go. I went home and slept on it and the next day found myself walking in and resigning, declaring that I could no longer continue to work in a place where I was not free. As I heard the words roll off my tongue, I felt as if I was in shock, standing outside my body and observing this enormous leap that I was taking!

In retrospect, I see that I had been protected from making this move until I was ready to do so. As I gained spiritual strength, my dissatisfaction had grown but my inner self was not yet strong or clear enough for me to go it alone successfully. In fact, my job had supported my spiritual re-awakening at this time because its financial security allowed me to explore my spirituality through the external world of workshops, books and tapes. However, after my sojourn in Sedona, my soul had strengthened and my exploration turned inward. When the universe decided I was ready to step into my true vocation, all the events around me conspired to make this happen. Interestingly, once I had taken my leap of faith by resigning, the universal life force immediately swooped in to support me. Even though I had given the required three months' notice, my boss, who was very in tune with me, decided not to look for my replacement for some time. I ended up staying for another nine months, which gave me all the time I needed to get used to my life-changing decision.

The best way to deal with your life changes is neither to fight them nor to force them. Instead, you will need to develop a strong belief that the universal intelligence is supporting you and knows better than you what is best for you. Sooner or later you'll have to relinquish control and allow these changes to take place in your life at the right time, trusting that the universal life force will not let you go backwards along your spiritual path. Equally, you cannot make your evolution go any faster than you are able to go yourself. At this point, trust in your newly developed powers of intuition and your deepened connection with your soul to carry you over these changes.

The Dark Night of the Soul

Before we move on to the more positive aspects of the transition period, there is one more potentially difficult episode that you may well encounter. The so-called 'dark night of the soul' is a time when we must go inside ourselves and face our fears. This dark place inside us is traditionally known as our 'shadow'. Perhaps the worst part of facing your shadow is that its presence usually comes as a very unpleasant surprise! Expressing our vulnerability is traditionally seen as a weakness (although this is gradually changing), so we have learned to suppress and conceal our pain and fears. Consequently, when you go inside and start to reconnect with your true self, you may well at first encounter feelings of shame at the pain you carry inside you. This is because your general life experience has indicated that feelings such as inadequacy, jealousy, guilt, anger, dishonesty and bigotry are inappropriate and unattractive. It has therefore stopped you examining the fear that lies behind them.

Facing your shadow involves waking up from a game of fear-based deception and deciding that you don't want to live that way any more. As you do this, the denial you had used to cover up your shadow may resurface in an attempt to stop you addressing it. At this time, remember that you are releasing the fears inside you to make yourself healthy and whole again. The greatest pain you can experience comes from trying to block this release. It's only when you stop denying your shadow self and agree to work with the transformational gifts it offers that you can begin to move away from it. For instance, you may realize that for years you have developed an acerbic wit to protect your vulnerability. Once you acknowledge this, you can catch yourself every time you are about to make a caustic remark to keep the world at bay. Instead, by lowering your defences you can allow your tenderness and compassion to be heard, and make others feel better about themselves at the same time.

The most important part of facing your shadow is that you forgive it and do not judge it. All human behaviour has a positive intention. Whatever you may have done in your life, you did it because on some level you thought it would make you feel better. With the limited resources available to you at the time, you were always doing what you believed would best ease your pain or gain you happiness. Also, don't expect your shadow to disappear completely! The human experience is one of duality and your weaknesses are all a part of who you are in this lifetime. By using your soul level awareness to remind you that your infinite self is filled with light and love, you will focus more and more on these aspects of yourself and gradually your shadow will retire into the background. From time to time, as any fears and pain resurface, honour them, understand them and do all that you can to transcend them through love and faith.

As part of this whole process, which is also known as a 'healing crisis', some people experience certain symptoms of detoxification. This is because your body starts spontaneously purging as you cast off years of negative habits and patterns. In much the same way that a physical detox can cause your skin to break out, the effect of your old fears and emotional toxins surfacing to leave your body can cause disruption to your entire system.

For example, emotionally you may find yourself much more ready to cry as you release years of suppressed sorrow. Although, at first, your tears may be those of pain, it's important to realize that crying is just another perfectly natural way of expressing intense emotion. Even after your healing crisis has passed, your increased sensitivity to life may cause you to shed tears of joy and gratitude at the overwhelming beauty, poignancy and power of the universe around you. Your increased compassion will also cause you to empathize with the tribulations and triumphs of others as your heart opens up to the oneness of the human condition.

Physically, you may suddenly discover that your body is more sensitive than you were aware of, or that you have allergies to certain foods or other environmental factors. I endured a lot of health problems during my dark night of the soul. They were created by the deep fear inside me that would wake me up in the middle of the night in a state of terror. During this time I felt a loneliness such as I had never known or, more accurately, a loneliness that I had stifled for years. After much inner turmoil, I came to understand that the only way I could deal with my terror and loneliness was to go inside and connect very strongly with my creator to ease my sense of separation and isolation. Even though this is the time when you may least feel like meditating, it is the time when you most need it.

The best way to deal with this period of your life is to step back a little from the world and take time to be gentle and caring with yourself. At this part of your journey to Spiritual Fitness you experience a rebirth into your true self. You are like a newborn baby and you need to nurture yourself lovingly while you pass through this stage of vulnerability. As we saw in WorkOut Two, you can help the process along by purifying your life as much as possible. To reiterate, cut down, (or if you can, cut out), all toxic substances, drink lots of water, eat healthy foods, take gentle exercise, get plenty of sleep and avoid people and situations that don't make you feel good. As you face your fears you will feel their illusion begin to dissolve. Eventually, your newly opened, fearless heart will expand outwards and reconnect you to the world as your naturally positive, vibrant and loving self. When in doubt, remember that it is always darkest before the dawn. No matter how unpleasant it may feel at the time, this intense period does end and you will emerge strong and clear as a radiant beacon to others. You'll also feel a sense of triumph and accomplishment and you'll possess an unassailable new level of self-understanding and wisdom.

TAKING THE LEAP OF FAITH

Gaining the momentum you need to take the leap of faith and live out your true purpose is a lot easier than you think. This is because, as you move into this new world of openness and trust, you will be operating at a much higher soul level. At this level you'll find you possess tools and resources inside you that you never knew you had. For example, your intuition will be so developed that you will instinctively know how to take timely and effective actions. Your connection with your soul and the universal life force will give you the deep faith that you are protected and guided and this will give you increased confidence. Your new-found ease with yourself will make your interactions with others smoother and more positive. So, let's now discover more about these resources and how you can use them to your best advantage.

Magnetism versus Manipulation

In the earlier stages of this course, we looked at the ways in which you could influence your external world through deliberate, conscious effort. We learned how you could get yourself motivated and influence others through conscious communication. Now that you have tuned yourself up into a much more sophisticated being, you'll find you have other powers at your disposal that require a lot less effort. When you advance to pure soul level living, the limitations of your former earth level strategies become apparent and you will find them pedestrian in comparison to the subtle yet powerful skills you have now developed.

Your new powers are a lot more feminine in nature. I don't mean this in a gender-based but in an energetic way, similar to the male and female aspects of electromagnetic force. The feminine way is to draw towards you what you want by the gravitational pull of your internal strength, while the masculine way is to go out and manipulate the world into fulfilling your wishes. It is because your new feminine powers soften your interactions with the world that many of your former tactics become redundant.

At this stage, people often become a little bemused when they see their old strategies no longer working. For instance, rigidity and controlled, fearful thinking may have once appeared to be the only tools you could rely on to get you through life – as you once believed it to be. You had your routine, your set opinions and your fixed responses to any issues that threatened to take you out of your familiar but static environment. Then one day you woke up and none of this seemed to make sense any more. The tools that you had were completely inappropriate to your new reality. You found that you are just as likely to achieve your dreams by meditating on them and preparing yourself to receive them as you are by going out and bludgeoning the world into making them come true! Your most powerful resources are now the very qualities you once thought most dangerous, because they seemed like the ones you could least control. These wonderful new gifts are your fluidity, spontaneity, openness and trust.

The effects of this more feminine, magnetic approach will soon begin to appear in your everyday life. Where you may previously have been a great planner and would have arranged months in advance how your life was going to be, now you can leave yourself more free time to allow the miracles of serendipitous events to occur. If you'd always needed to know exactly *how* you were going to achieve everything you wanted, you can start to accept that 'how' is none of your business. The universe is only too happy to take care of business on your behalf, while you are supposed to get on with enjoying your life and operating at as high a soul level as possible! To do this you will need the next tool, without which it is impossible for you to go any further along your path. You will need to have faith.

Faith

Many people come to faith as a last resort, often during or after their dark night of the soul. They will first try everything in their conscious power to make things happen the way they want and, when all else fails, they will have no alternative but to trust. For some, faith comes as the result of a dramatic experience, an epiphany, and for others it develops gradually. The whole point of faith is not so much *what* you believe in, as long as you perceive it as a loving, protective force, but the *extent* to which you believe in it. You may choose to believe in a god in the sky or in the fairies at the bottom your garden and, as long as your faith is absolute and all pervading, it will work. It's on this issue of all pervasiveness that many people stop short. Having dipped their toes into the deep waters of faith, they will trust enough to allow an 'angel' to find them a parking space. Yet when it comes to the more serious issues of finance or career, for example, they will prefer to take the matter into their own hands.

A Course In Miracles tells us that we cannot serve two masters. You can't have a bit of faith for the smaller things in life but none for the bigger ones. Faith is an absolute and as such it demands your complete belief in and obedience to a higher power. If you use faith in some areas of your life, and logic and fear-based reason in others, you will actually negate the effects of your faith throughout.

A woman who regularly attended one of my groups was happy to have faith for minor family issues but when the time came for her to set up her own business, she decided that faith was not enough and her old, structured strategies were what were needed most. I watched as her fears resurfaced and temporarily eclipsed the magic flow that had begun appearing in her life. Needless to say, things didn't work out as she so rigidly planned and eventually she had to acknowledge that maybe there was another way to do things. When she surrendered personal control and trusted the universe to guide her forward in the way that was best for her, things immediately began to work out for her.

Fortunately, faith is something that grows the more that you use it. As you see your prayers being answered and miracles occurring in your life, you will be encouraged to trust more and more deeply. Again, in *A Course In Miracles*, we learn that a miracle is a shift in perception and time and time again you will experience this shift happening in yourself and in those around you. For instance, you may have a friend who is in a very destructive relationship or who is addicted to alcohol or drugs. You may have spent endless days and nights trying to talk them out of their situation. Eventually you will decide on a new approach and, instead, just send them love and have faith that they will find what works for their highest good. When one day they call you and say they finally know why and how to move on, (assuming this is the best result for their soul's evolution at the time), you can give thanks for a miracle.

In my own life, I find that the more I trust, the more my faith is validated. I won't pretend that this is always easy and it is something that takes courage and focus. Even when things don't always turn out the way that I had hoped, in retrospect I can always see the divine order and perfection in the situation. When your faith blossoms into manifested reality, you feel an overwhelming sense of gratitude and a sublime connection with the universal life force.

Sensitivity

As your heart opens and you get more in touch with your real feelings, your overall sensitivity will increase. As people allow themselves to soften and their protective walls to crumble, they often become concerned that they will be laying themselves open to abuse from others. They fear that they may become emotional doormats or gullible pushovers. The truth is that as you become more sensitive, you become a lot stronger. Firstly, this is because you no longer have the debilitating disadvantage of trying to hide who you really are and secondly, because you have connected with a deep knowing that enables you to see through to the truth in others, no matter what façade they may be presenting to you. When you connect with your own and others' authenticity in this way, you become much more powerful and you automatically raise the level of your interactions.

I have encountered many everyday instances of the power of this raised vibration in my life. Several times, for example, I have watched as tradesmen have tried to charge me over the odds for services. Immediately I have been able to sense their anxiety as they 'try it on' and have also seen the fear and insecurity that lie behind this. So, in response, I simply hold my energy, smile sweetly and send them a silent vibe that says, 'I know what you're trying to do and I am sure that there's a greater level of integrity of which you are capable'. Then, as a miraculous shift of perception takes place inside them, I see them pull back and offer me a better deal. I also sense their relief that they have risen above their own smallness and are interacting from a more open-hearted place of integrity inside them.

As a further illustration of this, do you have in your life an acquaintance or a co-worker who you feel is always trying to belittle you? In the past, this might have caused you to keep up your protective walls. Then you would have related to them either by engaging in an earth level argument or by retreating into stony silence. With your new resource of heightened sensitivity, you will find you are able to raise your thinking up to a soul level and see that they are only acting in this way because deep down they feel so insignificant themselves. Now, instead, you can access your compassion and deep inner wisdom to find a way to deal directly with their insecurity.

Another wonderful by-product of your increased sensitivity is that it allows you to see the funny side of life! When you watch people get caught up in their earth level dementia, believing it to be real, it's often like watching children squabbling in the playground. You can see what they are trying to achieve and you know just how futile and irrelevant it all is in the greater scheme of things. Often the best approach to take towards the jibes of others is to imagine yourself literally head and shoulders above them, towering over them in the great playground of life. Learn to take yourself up to your full soul power and nobility and make your sensitive, real insights your greatest ally and strength.

Courage

Your magnetism, your faith and the silent power of your heightened sensitivity will make you feel a lot more confident and at peace within yourself. As you develop your authentic power in this way, you will gain courage. You will be ready to try things you may have been terrified of before, because you know that you can simply call upon a higher power and your deepest, inner resources to get you through. Increasingly, you will come to rely on your intuition and you'll find yourself making the right moves at the right time.

As you see yourself hitting the mark more and more often and getting positive results in your dealings, you will gain momentum. Your growing courage will thrust you forward until you trust enough to live your truth completely. For example, someone may offer you the opportunity to speak in public on a topic dear to your heart, yet in the past you had always been terrified of public speaking. By going inside and accessing your wisdom and courage, you'll find yourself accepting because you are more driven by the need to get your message across than by a limiting fear.

Your courage will enable you to take risks and become the person you have come here to be. It will set you free to step out of your old humdrum world of fear-based thinking and it will make you more creative, loving and trusting. Your courage will help you to make your unique contribution to the world and this in turn will fulfil you and bring you great peace and joy. So now that you are aware of your new set of resources, let's look at how you can find out what your special purpose is on Earth.

ANSWERING THE CALL

Each of us has come to this planet with a unique make-up and attendant set of gifts. To be gifted does not mean that you have to play the piano like Mozart or paint like Van Gogh. It means connecting with your core essence and discovering how you can make your own special contribution to the lives of others. My grandmother was a gifted woman in that she knew how to bring peace and joy to everyone through her smile. Some people are good listeners, others are helpers and some are here to inspire us. Your gift is simply the way in which you have come to bless the world with your presence.

Delivering this gift to the world is your purpose in life. One very important thing to remember about your purpose is that it is not necessarily the way by which you earn your living. Just because you can make people laugh doesn't mean you have to become a stand-up comic. Instead, it may mean that you realize you are supposed to touch the lives of those around you in a much more personal and tender, less contrived way. Native peoples, who didn't have to 'go to work' but lived their lives doing what came most easily to them, truly understood this concept. In cultures such as the Native American, each tribe member would be honoured for their natural abilities and identified with their particular gifts.

Finding Your Purpose

In modern day society, we define a great deal of our identity by the work that we do. Consequently, it's very common for people to feel, as they reconnect with their true selves, that their job no longer fulfils them because it doesn't represent who they really are. They may dream of doing something that they feel is more meaningful or of getting away from the 'rat race' and living in the middle of nowhere. While your inner development frequently necessitates a career change, this is not always so. Perhaps you are supposed to stay where you are and, as your inner strength grows, become a kind of spiritual infiltrator, a beacon of strength and authenticity, who helps and inspires those around you through your mere presence.

One of my greatest teachers, and someone I regard as a particularly enlightened being, works as a motorcycle courier by day. During this time, he comes into contact with many different people and is able to spread his light to them with his smile, his cheery disposition and his compassionate nature. At night, he runs free healing groups and so he truly understands that the power of selfless service is the best way for him to bless the world with his presence. In your case, it may be that withdrawing from society and keeping your light all to yourself is the way in which you *least* honour your gifts. Whatever the case, allow your intuition, deep wisdom and faith to guide you in the right direction.

Another commonly mistaken belief is that to live your purpose you must become a healer or open a healing centre. I often wonder what would happen if everybody did this, because surely then there would be nobody left to be healed! If you want to help others, remember that sometimes the greatest gift of healing you can give to someone is simply to sit and let them talk, or be affectionate to them or even clean up the chaos in their house. We all have a gift of healing which is nothing to do with certificates on a wall or with fancy rituals, but is rather the result of the peace, open-heartedness and hope that we can awaken in others. Some of the greatest healers I know are little children, who have no qualifications other than their pure, open and loving hearts.

So how do you discover just what your gift is? There is a saying that 'success leaves clues' and so it is with your life's purpose. If you want to know what your real gift is then look first at your childhood and you may find that whatever you were good at back then is a pointer to your soul's strength. For example, did people always comment on your sunny disposition? Were you particularly good at inspiring others, making them laugh or soothing away their troubles? Did you excel at something such as drawing, writing, talking or some kind of physical exercise? Take a moment now to think back and remember what kind of compliments you got or what you always did well as a child …

You may find that in doing this, you have suddenly remembered skills or activities that you haven't used or pursued for a long time. Or you may recall being praised for a particular aspect of your personality that you have since ignored.

When you arrive on this planet you are fresh from your all-knowing, infinite source, and you carry with you vestiges of memories of who you truly are and what it is that you have come here to do. The imaginary games that you played as a child and the roles that you took in them, the dreams you had of what you would like to be when you grew up and the things that you had the greatest aptitude for, all hold vital clues to your true purpose. Of course, your childhood talents don't just mean what you were good at in school. I once asked a woman what she was best at as a child and she said that all she could remember was being told that she talked too much! I pointed out to her that in her adult life she had become a very successful sales woman and so at least she was using this gift on an earthly level. Since then she has become an accomplished personal development trainer, turning her 'talking' skills into a soul level gift. As you reconnect with your soul's knowing, your earliest memories will begin to resurface and with them you may discover your gifts and purpose.

Sometimes the clues for your particular greatness are to be found in the thing to which you have the greatest resistance. I can recall being terrified of public speaking and yet every time I heard an inspirational speaker I would feel a tremendous urge inside me to rush onto the stage and join them. This inner conflict went on for years until I went on a Vision Quest retreat that was designed to help participants find, amongst other things, their life purpose. (A Vision Quest is a perfect way for you to access your life's purpose and you can learn how to find more information on Vision Quests at the end of this course).

As I sat alone out in nature for two days and a night, contemplating my life and its meaning, I heard a clear inner voice tell me that my purpose was 'to inspire people with my words written and spoken'. At the time this made little sense to me since I wasn't writing or running any groups. Yet the magic of finding your purpose is that once you discover and acknowledge it, the universal intelligence will bring you the opportunities to fulfil it. Some months later, I had set up a workshop for a friend of mine to run and there was a group of people signed up and ready to come along. Two days before the event, my friend returned from a trip to Greece and told me that, in a most bizarre incident, her wet hair had touched a bedside lamp and she had received a mild electric shock. She was temporarily deaf and dizzy and quite unable to run a workshop. Nevertheless, she assured me that I was more than capable of running it myself. If the universe hadn't stepped in with such a gift, I would never have thought myself ready enough to do so. There is an old saying that 'when the student is ready, the teacher will appear'. Equally, when you are ready, your awareness of your gifts will appear and along with them, your life's purpose.

Finally, the things that you enjoy the most, the passion that you sometimes feel inside your heart, will also let you know what it is that you have come here to do. Your purpose is no secret. It is the way that your soul wants to manifest joy in the world and as you connect more and more deeply with your soul, your purpose will emerge naturally and gracefully into your everyday life. The most important thing that you can do at this stage, like a pregnant mother waiting for the birth of her child, is to prepare yourself for its arrival.

Preparing for Your Purpose

Many people complain that nothing exciting ever happens in their lives and yet, if it does, they find themselves totally unable to cope with it! Perhaps they dream of finding their perfect partner yet when she or he turns up, they behave in ways that show they are far from ready for them because they haven't yet learned to deal with themselves. I came up with a clear illustration of this when one day I was walking along the road to catch a bus. Even though I was at least five minutes away from the bus stop, I found myself constantly looking around to see if a bus was coming. Whenever I turned and saw nothing coming, I found myself complaining that there is never a bus when you want one. While I ambled along in this way, filling my mind with negative thoughts, a bus sailed past me, arrived at the bus stop and left before I had been able to get there! My complaints and dissatisfaction had been completely worthless since I was nowhere near the bus stop when it arrived.

So it is with much that we ask for in our lives. We spend most of our time wondering when our dream love/home/job is going to arrive, yet all the time whatever we want is out there waiting for *us* to show up and not the other way around. The fact is that nothing will come to you until you are ready to receive it in a way that will empower you. As we have seen throughout this course, if you have not prepared yourself properly you will not be able to enjoy or manage the true exhilaration and power that accompany the success of achieving your dreams.

The best way to prepare for the arrival of your purpose is to start living your greatness and rid yourself of the limiting beliefs that have kept you feeling small. If not, you will have to look on helplessly as the stuff of your dreams slips through your hands. For instance, if you dream of having lots of money to use in a humanitarian way and yet somewhere deep down you have a belief that you aren't good or big enough to be financially abundant, the moment the money arrives you will spend it like water. You can see this happening over and over again with lottery winners, the majority of whom spend all their winnings within the first few years. Clearing out your limiting beliefs can be a long process but with constant vigilance, discipline and application you can manage to eliminate most of them.

Purification is also a very important part of your preparation. If you want to draw powerful new energy into your life, you must make yourself a clean enough receptacle to hold it. For example, I can assure you from experience that a hangover quickly cancels out psychic ability! As you train yourself to feel good through the purity of meditation, clear thinking and honest feelings, you'll also find that you don't need artificial ways of getting high. You will experience a natural exhilaration when your heart opens and connects you to your source and to the world around you. This will bring you the rewards of love, peace and joy in a way that is healthy and nourishing for you. At this point, you will be ready and able to live your purpose and take your leap of faith with confidence, strength and success.

REVIEW

All transition has a built-in crossover period that is like a spiritual adolescence. During this period you may well experience some confusion and pain as you move from the static security of your old world to the flowing freedom of your new life.

In this dark night of the soul, your buried fears may cause disruption to your physical, emotional or mental well-being as you turn to face them and release them. You can help yourself at this time by purifying your life as much as possible. Learn to make peace with your shadow as an aspect of your finite self and then focus intently on the love and light of your infinite self.

You will find that your power is changing into a more feminine, magnetic one. You will learn to achieve more by ostensibly doing less and by actually going within and strengthening yourself.

To proceed along your spiritual path you must have faith. Your sensitivity is one of your greatest strengths because it connects you to your, and everyone else's, authentic power. As you develop this power you will gain the courage to become the person you have come here to be.

Each one of us has a gift. Your gift is simply the way that you enhance the lives of others. Your purpose is to deliver this gift.

There are many clues to discovering your purpose and when you are ready, the universal life force will present it to you. In the meantime, it is necessary for you to prepare yourself by purifying your mind and body.

THE INNER WORKOUT

I Think back over your life to approximately one, five and ten years ago and for each stage, compare your level of wisdom and Spiritual Fitness with where it is now. For each period, pick out some key events and re-evaluate them from a soul level perspective. Ask yourself what you know and understand about them now that you didn't know and understand then. What have they taught you? How have they offered you the opportunity to set yourself free from fear and pain?

2 Take an honest look at some of your shadow qualities and write down what has been your positive intention for yourself behind them. For example, if you have been jealous of someone's good fortune, how have you used your jealousy to condemn them in your mind, thinking that this will make you feel less inadequate? If you have been intolerant of someone's weaknesses, how have you used this to avoid focusing on your own?

Once you have discovered the positive intention behind your negative feelings, come up with some alternative fearless and loving ways of making yourself feel better around these issues. For instance, discover how, by celebrating the success of others, you can share in their happiness and so achieve your own. Work out how you can feel strong and noble by helping others to express and overcome their vulnerability. This will in turn encourage you to express and overcome your own vulnerability.

3 Now that you have developed your sensitivity to such a degree, use it! For the next week, make a point of sensing the real motives behind the speech and actions of others. Then respond directly to these from your loving, strong and wise soul level perspective. If you do this consistently for a week, it will start to become second nature to you and you'll begin to let go of your old, less effective ways of interacting and you will just 'know' people by spending a few minutes with them.

4 Unearth your inner spiritual, emotional and financial gold mine. Begin by writing down three positive qualities that you felt were not given to you by your parents, (or those who raised you), in your childhood. Now review these qualities and know that these are *your* gifts. The reason they were missing from your upbringing is because they were the gifts that *you* brought to your family. Next make a list of at least three things that you *love* to do and are passionate about. Finally, list at least three things that you are good at, no matter how simple they may seem. Now put all of these three lists together and for the next week, allow your unconscious mind to present you with a way in which you can merge all or some of these natural resources to give you authentic, professional and/or emotional fulfilment.

5 Honour your purpose. Once you discover what it is, make it a conscious part of your identity and this will begin to strengthen it. If you feel, for example, that your purpose is to make people laugh, then learn some jokes! If you are a wonderful cook, start making meals for your friends and then you might even want to brighten up the lives of those who are less fortunate with your talents. In this way you can start to celebrate and enjoy your greatness.

HOLDING YOUR POWER & LIVING WITH JOY

**'Our greatest glory is not in never falling,
but in rising every time we fall.'**

Confucius

B y now there will be many aspects of this course that you will have absorbed, both consciously and subconsciously. Whichever techniques and concepts have most relevance for you will be the ones that you start to use in your life. As with all subjects, learning something and living it are two different things. *A Course In Miracles* tells us that the only way we truly learn anything is when we teach it, because to teach it authentically we also have to embody it. For you to stay spiritually fit, you will need to live your truth and constantly bring your soul level awareness into your everyday life. Spirituality is not just reserved for 'holy' moments. It is a way of living that involves the practical application of certain positive qualities and attitudes in *every* situation. When you consistently live this way, it will set you free and open you up to new levels of joy and peace in your life.

In this final WorkOut we'll look at how you can maintain your Spiritual Fitness and keep your spiritual awareness constantly nourished.

HOLDING YOUR POWER

As I stated at the very beginning of this course, Spiritual Fitness is not about being perfect. It is about constantly *aspiring* to a life of heart-filled integrity. Each day you will be presented with choices and challenges and invited to respond to them with your highest wisdom and your deepest faith. This occurs, not because the universal intelligence is trying to trick you, but because it always wants to ensure you are strong enough before you advance further on your ongoing journey. All structures that are built to be solid must be tested for their strength during their construction. For example, if you're building a chair you will put pressure on it as you create it to make sure that it can hold you. Similarly, you will regularly be invited to demonstrate your growing inner strength and power by being presented with forces of resistance. Your greatest task now is to learn how to hold your spiritual power throughout all the circumstances of your life and in order to do so you first need to understand the intrinsic make-up of this power.

Dealing with Heightened Sensitivity

As you step into full spiritual awareness, you'll discover that many of your basic tastes have changed. This can affect everything from your eating habits to the types of people you want around you, the ways that you choose to relax, and the things that excite and inspire you. These changes happen because you have become a much more re-fined mechanism. Your energy is lighter, you have raised your personal vibration to a higher frequency and, consequently, you connect with the world in a more delicate, balanced and accurate way. Precisely *because* you have become such a finely-tuned instrument, you will find that you must treat your mind, body and emotions with a new respect. One of my teachers frequently warned me about this, telling me that the higher I climbed spiritually, the further I had to fall if I engaged in too many negative, earth level pursuits. I could never quite grasp this concept until I came up with the following analogy.

So many of us go through life metaphorically driving an old jalopy, (how we live our lives). We dream of having a new and more powerful car but in the meantime we're quite comfortable moseying along in our familiar old heap. This tried and tested vehicle, (our secure but limiting world), enables us to drive in the sloppy fashion to which we have become accustomed, looking out of the window as we go and not really paying too much attention to where we're going or the speed at which we're getting there. The inside of this car may be strewn with years' worth of debris such as discarded food wrappings, loose change and dog-eared maps (our accumulated negativity), but we don't really notice it because we've got used to it that way. Then one day our dream comes true and we find ourselves behind the wheel of a brand new car equipped with all the latest technology and power steering. If you have driven a car with power steering you will know that 'sloppy' is no longer the way to go! Your slightest move dramatically turns the vehicle and your life is suddenly at risk if you don't give full attention to your speed and direction. You also notice that the inside of this car is very clean and it feels important that you keep it this way. To drop a food wrapper here would seem almost sacrilegious!

And so it is with your life. As you purify yourself, you'll become aware that your new 'tuned-up', cleansed and rarefied system is now more affected by any kind of toxicity in your environment. As you start to operate at a higher frequency, you will find that you can no longer get away with 'just one more' self-indulgent, obsessive thought, piece of junk food or drunken evening without subjecting yourself to imbalance. Of course, we are all on this planet to enjoy our lives and taking yourself too seriously as a 'spiritual being' and leading an existence of total self-denial has its own pitfalls. Often, when people first embark on their path of reawakening, they start to suffer from terminal seriousness syndrome! At its most extreme, this can lead you to a joyless life where none of your senses is fed with life's wonderful array of delights, so remember to bring laughter and fun and passion into all that you do.

As you settle into your new spiritual identity, you will become less earnest and realize that spirituality also means enjoying and appreciating all of the beauty of life. At this level of self-awareness, you become your own regulator and will be able to discern the difference between a junk food experience and a harmless indulgence, between savouring a fine glass of wine and rendering yourself numb to its pleasures through excess. You'll know exactly how much you can indulge yourself and how and when to pull back, recharge and balance yourself.

You will discover that your heightened awareness has its own rewards. For everything that you have given up, you'll find many healthier, more empowering alternatives given to you in their place. Addictive patterns such as dangerous, destructive relationships will eventually seem absurd and hold no attraction for you and you will draw to you those with whom you share mutual respect and a sense of light-heartedness. Miraculously, physical addictions such as alcohol and drugs will also hold no attraction for you. I can remember thinking that nothing on earth would be able to take away my urge for a drink when I was under stress and, indeed, nothing 'on earth' could. Yet, almost imperceptibly, as I strengthened my connection with my authentic self, I found alcohol less and less appealing until one day I woke up and my compulsive desire was gone. Remember, as long as you are addicted to anything you cannot be truly free, and freedom is essential for your spiritual well-being.

Understanding Energy

Another aspect of your new power is your enhanced awareness of energy. As you become increasingly aware of your own energy and how deeply places, people and situations affect you, you'll learn to take yourself away from situations that cause you fear, agitation or just sheer boredom! If a situation feels oppressive or draining to you, then, if possible, leave immediately. (If you can't physically leave, then practise withdrawing into your silent power, as discussed in the next section). Realize that you do not have to put up with negativity in your life. Seize your power and reject the things that do not make you feel good. The less you compromise on your need for peace and joy, the more the world will honour and fulfil these needs in you.

Also, you'll find that you are able to read the energy of others. Increasingly, as you engage with people, you may either experience physical sensations, an inner voice whispering in your ear, or unexpected visual images appearing before you. These will be transmitting to you the true information about the person with whom you are interacting and this may directly contradict the message they are consciously trying to give you. Remember to use your new, subtle awareness with compassion, otherwise it will give you an unfair advantage and upset the balance of your communication with others. Even those who have not yet spiritually re-awakened can pick up on smug superiority! So, when you encounter any fearful disguise in others, just show yourself to be warm and non-judgmental. The more open and loving that you are, the more open this will encourage them to be.

With your heightened awareness you will also start to sense the many dimensions of reality that exist simultaneously all around you. As we saw in WorkOut Five, your body has an electromagnetic energy field known as your etheric body or aura. Through your aura you are able to pick up many previously invisible energy fields in your environment. As you deepen your connection with your inner consciousness, you'll find that you can get a sense of people and events in advance. If you focus clearly enough, you will be able to pick up the energy of your own future, so you can prepare for the opportunities that are in store for you. For example, you will just *know* that the right job or partner is on their way and, as you become more adept, you will even know when this is likely to happen.

Your new awareness can be used to help you find the answers to your most soul-searching questions. A very powerful technique to achieve this is to write a brief letter to your soul or the universal life force, asking it a simple question. Then, immediately write back to yourself *without thinking about it* and you'll be amazed at the accurate and helpful insights that you receive. The most important thing here is that you learn to trust your own intuition.

As you begin to operate solely at this soul level of awareness, you may at first find that there are few people who share your deep under-standing of life and who are able to offer you support. (This is com-pensated by the fact that those who do will form deep connections with you and significantly enrich your life. Eventually you will draw to you a wide circle of like-minded souls.) To maintain your Spiritual Fitness in the everyday world, you'll need to go within and develop your own methods to conserve and top up your energy anywhere and at any time.

Conserving Your Energy

As you deepen your understanding of energy, you will develop an inner knowing of when to act and when to be still. For instance, where in the past you may have responded to every remark that was made to you, you now know when and how to stay silent and hold your power. Your silent power is one of your greatest resources and is an essential part of Spiritual Fitness. We live in a culture where our words, like so much else, have become throwaway items. So many people chatter mindlessly, drowning out the reflective power of silence. As you learn to keep your own counsel, you give yourself the time and space to glimpse new insights that you would otherwise have missed.

In a similar manner, you can learn to conserve energy by making yourself invisible. If you find yourself in a situation where you are surrounded by much negativity and you must stay in that place, learn to withdraw your energy from it. For example, if you're at a social gath-ering where there is a lot of aggression being expressed, to prevent yourself being harmed by the negative energy that is flying around, withdraw your awareness inside yourself and be as still as possible. Using any of the meditative techniques that work for you, build up your own energy until you are able silently to radiate a strong, peaceful vibration to those around you. Remember to do this with detachment and without expectations. As we have seen throughout this course, expectations and judgments will always unsettle your inner peace and drain your energy. Just know that, at a soul level, your lighter vibration may take some time to filter down through the negative energy of those around you and it may or may not have an obvious effect. Nevertheless, you will be able to maintain your serenity and balance. Practising the art of invisibility and compassionate detachment is an essential tool for holding your power.

Conserving your spiritual energy also means realizing that you do not owe the world an explanation for your actions or inaction. At this level of self-mastery, you must be able to hold your power without feeling beholden to those around you or trying to gain their approval. For instance, do you have a friend who repeatedly asks you to lend them money but never uses it for anything constructive? You may find yourself torn between the earth level guilt of wanting to help them out on a short-term basis and knowing, on a soul level, that the most empowering option for them would be to discover how to create their own wealth. So, instead of wearing yourself out worrying over what you should 'do', you can simply choose to do nothing and not lend them any money *without necessarily needing to explain why*. If you feel that you can reach them by telling them your honest reasons, then do so. Otherwise remain still and silent in your actions. Your own understanding of your sincerity and integrity is enough.

In conserving your spiritual energy it is important to avoid any unnecessary waste of your physical energy. Since your body is your soul's vehicle for the duration of your stay on Earth, you need to keep it strong and rested. Many people get caught up in frenzied physical activity simply out of habit. Look at your life closely and ask yourself how much of your time is taken up by self-prescribed duties and obligations. For instance, do you have routine times for shopping, cooking, cleaning or socializing to which you have until now rigidly adhered?

Free yourself from your own rules and do only what needs to be done *when* it needs to be done. If your cupboard is already full, take a rest from food shopping and live off your supplies. Instead of cooking every day, spend a few solid hours preparing several meals in advance. Clean when it is necessary and not just because it's cleaning day. And, if you've been out with friends for most of the week, don't feel obliged to go out once more just because it's Friday night. The time and energy that you conserve will enable you to do some of the things that your soul really wants to do.

By going inside and holding your stillness, you will build up powerful, concentrated energy. Masters of martial arts have a deep understanding of this concept. I once heard of an Eastern master who was able to break a thick piece of wood with only two fingers and cut the top clean off a bottle with a slice of his hand. In both of these cases, he moved suddenly from apparent inertia to quick, decisive action and then, just as quickly, returned to stillness again. Within his stillness he had built up such a tremendous force of energy that he was able to demonstrate through his actions the power and effectiveness of perfect focus and minimal, concentrated effort.

Becoming a Beacon of Light

As your inner light grows ever stronger, you'll find that you draw to you people who will try to bask in your light instead of doing anything to access their own. Your greatest gift to these people is to encourage them to step into their own power instead of using your greatness as an excuse to hide from theirs. If anyone tries to give their power to you, elevating you above themselves, gently but firmly refuse to accept it. For instance, if there's someone who seems unable to make a decision without asking your opinion first, you must eventually help them by remaining silent and making them trust their own inner wisdom. At all times, avoid allowing your ego to take these situations personally and give you a false sense of superiority which will immediately draw you out of your authentic power. Recognize, instead, that they result from other people's fear of assuming their own power.

All human interactions are based on a struggle between light and dark, between who is less afraid and who is more afraid. Your role as a beacon of light is to remain strong and inspire those who are yet to step out of their fear. If you are to help those around you *and* maintain your level of Spiritual Fitness at the same time you'll need to remember that you can't rescue anyone from quicksand by jumping in as well. You must stand firm on the side and pull them towards you. The more that you acknowledge someone's fears, the more real they become for the two of you. Instead, focus on the light so that it can grow.

I learned the truth of this with a woman who once came to me. She was an alcoholic and she assumed that I would want to know all the negative results of her drinking. Instead, I asked her to talk about what she had been proud of in her life. I refused to jump into the quicksand with her and engage in her familiar game of playing small and out of control. Each time she came to see me we continually focused on the light and strength in her that had been trapped and buried for so long. I showed her ways to connect with her soul on a daily basis and, slowly but surely, she began to pull away from drinking and into a fulfilled life. This was because, as her increasingly purified self began to under-stand the futile and damaging artificiality of being drunk, her light be-came more attractive to her than her darkness. She became her own beacon, pulling herself out of the quicksand.

In your role of service to others, you must also realize that you can only give so much of yourself. Each of us has a vital store of reserve energy that is intended only for our personal use. If you start to give this away, all your efforts will be counterproductive and you'll find yourself exhausted. I have observed many newly re-awakened souls, myself included, giving their energy to others until they are com-pletely empty themselves. Often we do this because deep down we feel unable or unworthy to hold the new power that we have and so we try to give it all away. As you grow more accustomed to your inner strength, and as your self-love and self-esteem grow with it, you'll learn just how much energy you need to keep for yourself. In the same way, you'll come to understand how much time you need to spend alone, how much in a neutral state with people and how much in a consciously giving mode.

Nature – the Great Restorer

The greatest way to revitalize and replenish your energy is by spending time in nature, preferably the type of landscape you find most attractive. Nature holds such a restorative power for us because we are children of this earth. Our bodies are made up of the materials of this planet and while we are here, our souls communicate with the universal life force through our minds and bodies. Nature has a primal, parental role in our lives and it is essential that you honour this if you are to maintain your heightened level of spiritual awareness.

When you encounter a breathtaking natural landscape, such as the awesome red rock mountains of Sedona, the torrential cascades of Niagara Falls, the towering giant redwoods of ancient forests or the exquisite underwater world of the Great Barrier Reef, you also connect with the majesty, beauty and vastness that they reflect inside you. Your soul expands as your inner landscape echoes and mirrors the outer landscape. At the same time your body relaxes and loosens up because it no longer feels constricted by the pressures of the unnatural world that most of us live in.

It is in nature that you can feel the universal life force most keenly. Here you will find the evidence that all of life is cyclical, a constant process of change – birth, death and rebirth. When I go on Vision Quests and spend days and nights in sole contemplation of the landscape around me, I understand the true healing power of nature. I have learned to take my problems to the ancient wisdom of the mountains and the limitless sky and, without giving my issues any more thought, I simply lie back and receive the healing that the eternal force of nature offers. I always find that, when I leave, my heart has been lifted and healed and I have new and effective insights into my life issues that have been imparted to me without any conscious effort on my part.

As you become more in tune with nature, you will come to recognize its symbols and the way that it uses them to communicate with you. A subtle breeze, the gentle swaying of the trees, birds that soar overhead or the ever-changing patterns of the sky all speak to you with messages from the universal intelligence. Whatever these messages mean to *you* is their true meaning since two people may have two very different interpretations of these natural signs. Your heart will tell you what is true as you become increasingly aware of your oneness with the universal consciousness. Within the seasons and cycles of nature you will also connect with your own cycles and learn when is the right time for you to move outwards to the world and when to withdraw into yourself for restoration.

Creating Everyday Sacredness

We each have certain triggers that awaken in us a sense of the sacred. For me it is the smell of burning sage such as the Native Americans use for purification. For others it may be a certain type of music, an image or icon, the burning of candles or the power of absolute silence. When you have discovered whatever works for you, then incorporate it into a daily ritual that will help to ground you in your spiritual awareness. For example, let some of your first and last thoughts each day consciously connect you with the universal life force.

You can use these triggers for an emergency boost and re-alignment with your soul. For instance, if you're in the middle of the city in a very stressful situation, close your eyes for a few moments and imagine your particular source of spiritual inspiration. Carry with you a photo or a memento of the place on Earth that you find most sacred. If there is a particular fragrance that you have come to associate with your times of deep inner peace and spiritual connection, keep a sample of it with you so that as you inhale it, you are transported back into this state of calm.

There is no place on Earth or in this universe where the universal life force cannot be found. To access it all you have to do is to invoke and tune into it. If you treat whatever name you give this force with great reverence it will give this word or phrase more power so that, whenever you use it, you will spontaneously enter into an altered state of sacred awareness.

LIVING WITH JOY

Once you understand the nature of the power that is now at your disposal, you will realize that you are a co-creator with the universal intelligence of your own life and destiny. You can literally start to create your own happiness. You'll see that you are now living at a level of self-mastery and it is up to you to follow your own rules and design your life. Eventually, all experts become masters of the methods they use and then they use their own creativity to become outstanding in their fields. Once you have grasped the basic skills of Spiritual Fitness, you will also find that you have less need of 'teachers' in your life. As you leave behind your spiritual adolescence you will blossom into your fully empowered, integrated self. You'll learn to trust and follow your own inner guidance and this will give you an exhilarating, and previously unimaginable, sense of freedom, power and joy. As this is an on-going process, there are certain qualities and attitudes that will always be essential to you. We shall now pull together all the strands of this course and distil these qualities into seven essential principles.

The Seven Principles of Spiritual Fitness

I DISCIPLINE

Unhappiness is a bad habit! To live your life joyfully and to your fullest potential you'll need the discipline to break the old, unconscious patterns that lead you back to self-doubt and discomfort. As you get a clearer overview of your life, you'll realize that all your experiences have been the result of choices that you have made. Now you will need to be continually vigilant that your future choices are based not on whatever gives you a short term fix but on what serves your highest good. Just as with all fitness programmes, Spiritual Fitness needs the discipline of tenacity, commitment and focus to stretch you constantly beyond your previous limitations.

As you progress, you'll soon come to realize that the everyday world in which most of us live is not necessarily set up to support the discipline of following your spiritual path. We are forever being tempted or forced into connecting with life at the level of the lowest common denominator. It's only too easy to come home at night, eat a ready-made meal and sit in front of the TV, or engage in mindless activities. To become a master of Spiritual Fitness you must break out and forge your own path. Start to question how much of your behaviour is spontaneous and creative and use your self-discipline to set yourself free.

You'll also need to discipline yourself to connect with the life-giving, creative force of the universe every day. Do this in whatever way works for you, for instance, by meditating or spending time in nature. Remember that to be good at anything, you need to practise it often. Many people imagine that once they engage on a spiritual path, everything in their garden will be rosy. They visualize a utopian life of peace and harmony, the perfectly fulfilling job, the perfectly loving relationship, the perfectly blissful state of mind. While all of these are attainable, to reap the rewards of Spiritual Fitness you must apply yourself to it with total dedication. Heaven takes practice and practice needs discipline.

2 AUTHENTICITY

Without truth as your anchor you are completely lost. All of the concepts and exercises in this course are based on your authentic expression of yourself. Your authentic self is you at your most raw, un-guarded and unencumbered. When you present this part of yourself to the world, doors will magically open for you. This is because there are many pathways available to you and they can all lead you to learning and growth. Some are like bumpy country roads that twist and turn. They will eventually help you to make progress but your journey will be difficult. Others are bland and unexciting and they will give you a similar experience of life! But there is one pathway that is designed just for you and if you take it, you will fast track to Spiritual Fitness and joyful living. The secret of this path is that it is cut exactly to fit your contour and this means that you cannot carry with you any baggage as you move along it. And so, to enter into the clear flow of life that is waiting just for you, you must live in the moment as your free, authentic self, unfettered by past conditioning or fearful, self-defensive behaviour. All great spiritual leaders have shared this authenticity and lack of guile. It involves remembering that everyone on this planet is an eternal soul in human form.

So that people can really experience this, in my WorkOut Groups I often give them hugging lessons. I tell them how the perfunctory hugs that we so often give each other may as well be handshakes from an energy point of view. Then I demonstrate a 'real' hug that entails con-necting your whole body with your hugging partner and dissolving into the infinite stillness that you share. For the first few seconds you usually feel awkwardness as you experience all the social taboos that have taught you to associate close physical contact with invasive or sexually suggestive behaviour. As you move through this feeling and allow it to subside, you will feel an exquisite blending of energies, in-tense relief and release, and an all-compassing soul love for your part-ner. It is in this soul connection that you will both find your most authentic selves.

Being consistent with your truth is also an essential part of your authentic power. Once you have discovered who you truly are, what you want from life and what you have come here to contribute, you won't be happy if you settle for anything less than absolute truth in your life. Compromise will become as painful to you as it was once numbing. As you understand your real needs and desires, adapt your lifestyle so you can wake up every morning and look forward to the day ahead. Happiness is your most natural state and if you are prepared to listen, your authentic self will guide you to the people, places and situations that bring you most joy.

3 FOCUS

The more that you open yourself up to living with expanded consciousness, the more focused and grounded you need to be. In fact, staying grounded is vital for Spiritual Fitness. For the duration of your stay on this planet, you need to have a good working relationship with Earth's everyday, three-dimensional reality. Otherwise you run the risk of becoming a destitute dreamer, 'off with the fairies'! Throughout your lifetime you have to eat, be sheltered and pay your way. Focus gives you powerful and protective discernment as you withdraw from the tribal perception of reality but still have to abide by some of its rules. It allows you to integrate effectively the many dimensions of reality that you are now aware you inhabit.

During and after all of your interactions with those around you, you must return to your centre as quickly as possible. No matter how far you have to stretch out of your stillness, into the mayhem around you, you must return to your inner peace or anchor. Otherwise, you will begin to float adrift in the sea of others' emotions and fears. Focus also means simplifying and distilling every situation down to its core essence and only dealing with that most real aspect of it.

4 FLEXIBILITY

Your flexibility is the route through which the universal life force is able to guide and support you. It is only by making a space for this force of change in your life that you can allow it to surprise you with new, stimulating and life-affirming gifts. No matter how you think your future should look, there is often a better outcome, a more healing solution or a more positive direction being offered to you. Being flexible means responding to the energies around you and being ready to act on the information they give to you. Or you can use your flexibility to know when your current strategies aren't working and be prepared to alter them. Make changing your mind a luxury you can afford and you will allow the grace of the universal intelligence to bring miracles into your life.

Flexibility allows you to be completely present in each moment and to appreciate its newness. This will fill you with the wonder and zest for life of a small child. Toddlers just 'show up' at each new experience, unencumbered and endlessly curious. In return they are perpetually fascinated and excited by life and this is a gift that is available to you. Flexibility also enhances your creativity as you open up your mind and emotions to new ways of experiencing life.

5 TRUST

Belief is the fuel that manifests miracles and trust is one of the essential components of Spiritual Fitness. As you move further along your path, there will be times when you feel that you have no one to trust but yourself and your higher power. There will also be times when everything in your outer world seems to contradict the advice that you are being given by your inner self. At these times, you must trust and learn to follow your inner knowing regardless of external appearances.

To achieve this level of absolute trust, you have to live in a state of complete obedience and surrender to your higher power. Questioning your inner guidance will slow down or even stop the flow of help and protection that is available to you. When you are uncertain about what life has in store for you, you may find yourself turning to any methods of divination, such as tarot, to help you. When you doubt your future in this way, you are affirming to the universe your lack of faith and trust. As you become more adept at connecting with the universal intelligence, you'll start to believe that your prayers will be answered and then you can get on with enjoying your life in the certainty that a positive future awaits you.

Faith is the spiritual equivalent of physical energy. The more you tone up your ability to trust, the more you will find you have an abundance of confidence that enables you to do things you would never have previously dreamed possible.

6 PATIENCE

Be patient. All good things come to those who wait. For as long as you have been on this planet, you have been programmed with fear and mistaken thinking. The odds are that to release this and turn your life around will take more than a week or two! *A Course In Miracles* tells us that infinite patience brings immediate rewards. This means that as soon as you start to think at a soul level, you can sit back and allow life's events to unfold in their perfect divine order while you get the immediate reward of instant peace.

Gratitude is an important ingredient of your ability to be patient. As you wait for your dream home/job/partner to arrive, if you learn to give thanks for all that you have in your life right now, you release yourself from the tension of expectation and free yourself up to enjoy the pleasure of each moment. You must also learn to develop stamina and perseverance. It has been said that the major part of success is simply showing up. If you can stick around and show up for all the auditions in your life, sooner or later you will be given the role that is right for you.

7 LOVE

Of all of the components of Spiritual Fitness, love is the most important and the most powerful. As the saying goes, love is what makes the world go around. It is the visible manifestation of the universal life force and it includes such qualities as kindness, warmth, understanding, generosity and tenderness. The more spiritually fit you become, the more you will feel the warm, fluid energy of love suffuse your whole being.

Love is the only way that we can hope to reach, heal and connect with one another. Throughout time, it has ultimately triumphed over the forces of darkness and fear and will continue to do so because it is real. Since there is a global re-awakening taking place on our planet, we are now living at the perfect time for everyone to wake up to this. Perhaps you have already noticed people in your life who are softening and undergoing a positive transformation that you would have previously thought impossible. Of course, the same process is happening to you. In the coming years, we will see the many aspects of love appearing more and more in our daily lives.

The good feelings that you experience when you have brightened someone's day with a smile, compliment or a helping hand or when you have received any of these gifts yourself, show you the meaning of love. The devotion that drives lovers to overcome seemingly insurmountable obstacles to be together, that compels parents to scale previously unsurpassable heights for their children or makes friends stick together through thick and thin, speaks to us of the power of love. The joy that you feel when someone sees you for who you truly are and acknowledges your essential beauty, radiates within you the warmth of love. Only in love can we find redemption from all the falsehoods that we have been living. Love is the gift that the universal life force has given to us free and in total, eternal abundance.

REVIEW

True spirituality is not reserved for 'holy' moments but is a continuous process of life awareness.

To learn to hold your spiritual power, you must honour the new, refined mechanism that is you and learn to regulate your behaviour in accordance with your increased sensitivity.

Conserve your energy and start to use your silent power.

Understand your responsibility to others as a beacon and learn to protect and enhance your light.

Nature is your great healer and restorer and it will teach you of the eternal cycles of life. Find ways to inspire your sense of the sacred in your everyday life.

Realize the value and the gift of each experience.

To be spiritually fit and live with joy, you will need to use the seven essential principles of Spiritual Fitness – discipline, authenticity, focus, flexibility, trust, patience and love. Love is the most important aspect of your life.

THE INNER WORKOUT

1   Each day when you wake up, decide on one positive quality that you want to bring into your life, such as communication, love, faith or creativity and make it your focal point for the day. You will usually find that within a few hours you are presented with invitations to overcome obstacles to this quality and to manifest it in your every day life. Then, at the end of the day, look back and notice how much you were able to draw that quality into your world.

2   Make a list of the ten things that bring you the most joy. Make it your goal to incorporate at least one of them into your life every day.

3 Imagine that you have left this world and, as your best friend, you are writing your epitaph. Write about yourself, in the third person, as you want to be remembered, mentioning your true gifts and real achievements, *whether or not you feel these have yet manifested in your life.* Keep this epitaph and check on it from time to time to make sure that you are becoming the person you truly want to be.

4 When you put this book down, go and find someone who will practise real hugging with you! Look for an open soul, explain to them what you want to achieve, (a deep, innocent and authentically loving soul connection), then when you hug, let yourself dissolve until your two souls merge together and you can truly feel the oneness of all life and the presence of the universal life force in all things.

AFTERWORD

As you have passed through this course, you have been given many opportunities to open yourself up to new levels of consciousness and understanding. Your spiritual need for faith and meaning has been acknowledged and guided. How much you choose to accept and develop this is now entirely up to you. Just remember that it is impossible for you to unlearn what you have discovered. No matter how much you may sometimes wander from your path of spiritual re-awakening, you will always carry inside you the insights and wisdom that you have already gained. And if you stay on this path, your world will open up and reveal its true, awesome beauty to you. You will realize that you are becoming increasingly loving and kind, free, honest, wise, at peace and joyful!

Always remember that you have come to this planet to bless the world with your own unique contribution and that who you are is enough. All that you need is already inside you. It is in the giving of your gift, in living your true purpose and receiving in return the bountiful rewards of life's rich experiences that you will find true fulfilment and joy. You will discover that the secret of Spiritual Fitness is to ask not what life can do for you, but what you can do for life. Enjoy your life and may you be blessed on every step of your sacred, eternal journey.

ABOUT THE AUTHOR

Caroline Reynolds is a Spiritual Fitness trainer and Celtic word-smith. She was born and raised in South Wales and is now based in London. She spends much of her time in her spiritual home of Sedona, Arizona where she regularly leads retreats and Vision Quests. Caroline is the author of *Thought Seeds For Growth*, a small book of insights which is available through her website. She has also created innovative meditation tapes with Terry Disley, composer and musician with Grammy nominated jazz group, Acoustic Alchemy.

For more information on Caroline's international workshops, lectures, retreats, tapes and Spiritual Fitness WorkOut Groups, please visit her website at:

www.spiritual-fitness.com or www.caroline-reynolds.com
E-mail: caroline@spiritual-fitness.com
Telephone:
+44 (0) 208 248 3655 (UK)
and
(1) 520 203 4660 (US)

INDEX

absurdity xxi
addictions 145
adolescence, spiritual 119–21
affirmations 61–2
alignment, with centre 37
   see also non-alignment
altars 37–8, 100
anger 52
archetypes 81
arguments 51–3
assertiveness 36
attacks, by others 6, 52, 53, 131–2
attitude, changing 21
aura 146
authenticity xii–xiii, 23, 34, 81,
   155–6
automatic thinking 26
awareness:
   inner xiv–xv, 97
   spiritual xiv
awkwardness, avoiding 59

baggage, emotional 28, 155
beacon of light 149–51
belief 157
belief systems 26–7
   for decisions 60
   examination 21–2
   negative, dissolving 27–30
   see also faith
bowls, singing 107
breath, and meditation 100, 102–5

chakras 110–14
challenges 64
change:
   acceptance 2, 3–5
   in basic tastes 143
   catalysts for 2–3, 74
   inevitability of 122–4
   and ingrained habits 29–30
   in modern life xiv
   in soul mate challenges 84–5
chanting 106–7

choices:
    and beliefs 27–8
    and change 122–4
    and forgiveness 30–31
    mental 25
circle of life xvii, 7
clear, being 20
colours 99, 110
comfort zone see familiarity
commiseration 58
communication see language
compassion 126, 132, 144, 148
competitiveness 120–21
compromise 156
connection:
    with higher power xii, xv, 88, 124,
        127
    need for 69–72, 147
consciousness, altered state 103
consequences, review 30
contemplation, creative xvi–xvii
control:
    ownership in 77–8
    taking 13
conversation 47
    gossip in 50
counting your breath 100, 104–5
courage 132–3
A Course in Miracles xxi, 2, 27, 130,
        142, 158
crises xxi, 2–3
crying 126
cycles of nature 39, 151–2
    see also circle of life

dark night of the soul 124–7, 129
decisions 60–61, 122–4
desire, and change 3, 11, 74
despair 3, 74
detachment 7, 148
detox, process 25–42
disappointment 11, 12
discipline 154

disempowerment 13
displacement activities 2, 5
dissatisfaction 122–4
dreams:
    expression 57
    realization xiv
drinks 42
drums 107–8

earth level thinking xix
emotions, clearing 32–4
encouragement, mutual xv
end, of relationship 72–4
energy 20
    conservation 147–9
    drainage channels 33–4, 145–6,
        148
    loss:
        through competition 120
        and gossip 50
    and meditation 101
    negative, in arguments 51, 52
    physical, waste 148
    reserve of 150–51
    understanding 145–7
environment:
    changing 23
    detoxing 36–40
    influences from 22, 33
    sacred, creating 100–101
envy 6
Erickson, Milton 103
etheric body 146
excess, and imbalance 144–5
exercise 42
expectations 7, 148
experiences:
    as enrichment 7
    equation 26–7, 30
    and language 48–9
    observer effect 95–6
experimentation 120
explanations, unnecessary 148

failure, fear of 7–9
faith xii, 129–31, 158
    leap of 127–33
familiarity 2, 3, 4, 7, 144
fear 1–9, 32, 52, 55, 72, 73
    facing 124–7, 129
    help for 150
    and negativity 150
    unresolved, and relationships 78
    see also individual fears
feelings, receiving 33–4
feng shui 25–7, 40
Findhorn xv
flexibility 157
focus 109, 156
food 35–6, 42
forgiveness 30–31, 125
free will 93
freedom 77–8
    through forgiveness 31
    vs addiction 145
friends 51, 58
    see also like-minded souls
future:
    divination 158
    feeling for 146

gift, special, contributing 133–8
goals:
    deliverable 9
    surrendering 12–13
gossip 49–51
gratitude 158
greatness, own, fear of 4–7, 32
    and freedom 78
    and mirroring 82
    and negativity 28
    and purpose 134–7, 138
    and relationships 80
grounding 156
growth:
    environment for 39–40
    and relationships 78

rewards of 24–5
sources of 7, 74

habits 148–9
    beliefs as 29–30
    and stuck feelings 38–9
happiness 156
harm, avoiding 35
Hay, Louise 108
healing 134–5
healing crisis 126
health problems 11, 126
higher power:
    connection with xii, xv, 88, 124,
        127
    guidance from xiii, 2
    surrender to 157–8
    voice of 56
home, layout 40
honesty 22–3, 24, 61
houseguests 38
hugging 59–60, 155

image, mirroring action 22
inadequacy, in others 6
infinity 96
inner self 91–7
inner voices 37, 54–6
inner workouts:
    1. Motivation recharge 15–18
    2. Soul detox 43–5
    3. Minding your language 66–7
    4. The relationship equation
        89–90
    5. Learning to meditate 115–17
    6. Taking the leap and finding
        your purpose 139–41
    7. Holding your purpose and
        living with joy 160–61
inner world, exploring 91–7
intent, declarations of 61
intuition 34, 56, 97, 124, 127,
    146–7

journey of self-discovery xi, xiii, xix, xxii
joy, living with 153–9
judgements:
    and gossip 50, 51
    moving away from 97, 146
    negative 31
    and safe responses 53

karma 86
kindness xviii–xix

landscapes 39–40, 151
language 46–67
laughter 35, 144
leap of faith 127–33
let it go/flow 64–5
lifestyle xiii, 142
light 110, 149–51
like-minded souls xv, 58, 147
Linn, Denise 108
loss, of relationship 72–4
love xviii, 32–3, 52, 68–90, 159
lying 59–60

magnanimity 7
magnetism 128–9
mandalas 109
manipulation 128–9
mantras 61–2, 99–100, 105–6
material things 12, 13
meaning:
    through language 47–9
    of life xii
meditation 36, 91–117
    method 98–103
    techniques 103–10
messages, contradictory 146
mind:
    feng shui for 25–7
    stilling 103, 149–51, 156
miracles 157
mirroring:

own image 22
in relationships 78–83
motivation 1–18
music 37, 101

nature 151–3
negativity:
    and choice of confidant 121
    clearing 20–21
    rejection 146, 147–8
    see also shadow feelings
New Age language 63–5
'no', saying 58–60, 148
non-alignment fatigue 34, 59
numbness 4

object, focusing on 109
old world, effects of change 23–4
'Oprah', playing 57
outcome:
    clear identification 9
    positive 30

pain:
    avoiding 11, 22
    healing closure 31
    as motivation 22, 73
pantomime approach 5
partners 68–90
patience 158
payoff 11–12
    and relationships 80
peace:
    choice of 31
    inner xvii, 93, 95, 156
personality, whole self in 81–2
place see environment
planning 129
positive reframing 57
positivity:
    in language 61-3
    and procrastination 8
    welcoming 21

posture, for meditation 101–2
poverty 11
power:
    holding 143–53
    personal 61
preparation, for purpose 137–8
procrastination 8–9
projection, in relationships 78–81
promises, feasible 9
psychotherapy 4–5
purification 19–45, 127, 138, 144
purpose, finding 133–8

reincarnation 86
reality, external, subjective
        interpretation of 95–6
reality, in self *see* authenticity
rebirth 127
reframing, positive 57
relationships 68–90
    avoiding 11
    perspective on 28
    success in, laws 75–8
    and surrender 12–13
    and trust 60
release 125
resonate 65
respect 76–7
responsibility 6, 51
rhythm:
    internal 102–3
    unique 120
risk-taking 133
road rage 48–9
role, one-dimensional 23
romance 71

sacred place, picturing 108–9
sacred symbols 109
sacredness 92, 152–3
Satir, Virginia 2
Seasonal Affective Disorder 39
self, total 23

self-criticism, avoiding 54–6
self-discovery 22
    see also journey of self-discovery
self-love 75–6, 77
    healing through 35–6
self-talk:
    negative 54–6
    positive 56–8
self-worth 35
sensitivity 20–22, 131–2, 143–5
seriousness 144–5
sex 40–41, 82–3
shadow feelings 32
    embracing 64
    facing 124–7, 129
sharing 121
silence:
    in actions 147–8
    healing through 37–8
    power of 92–3
simplicity xvii
singing bowls 107
single state 87–8
solitude 37–8, 92
soul, connection with 93
soul level thinking xix–xx, 5
    and peace 95, 97
    and relationships 72–4, 78
soul mates 83–6
souls, eternal xix
sound, and meditation 101, 105–8
space:
    experience of 96
    sense of 37
spirals 109
spiritual fitness:
    definition xi–xiv
    seven principles 154–9
spontaneity, healing through 38–9
start:
    making 1–2, 8–9
    small initial steps 9, 10, 14–15

statements:
  negative:
    avoiding 62–3
    lessening effect of 62
    positive 61–2
stillness 103, 149–51, 156
stress xiii, xvi, xvii
stuck feelings, and habits 38–9
subconscious mind 96
  images from 63
  and procrastination 8
subjectivity 95–6
success 6, 8, 32, 158
superiority, false sense 149–50
support, mutual 71, 77, 147
surrender 12–13
swearing 53–4
symbols, sacred 109

talents, childhood 135–6
tapes, for meditation 108
thoughts:
  disempowering patterns 25–6,
    95
  examination 21–2
  visual/auditory/kinesthetic types
    98–9
  vs knowing 97
  see also soul level thinking
time 96
  and inner clock 40
touch 47
Transcendental Meditation 99, 106
transition period 119–27

triggers 48, 152–3
trust 124, 129, 130, 157–8
truth 23, 59–60, 155

unhappiness 154
universal life force 127, 151–3, 159
unknown, fear of 1–4

Vision Quests 136, 151
visualization 108–10

wealth 12
weather 39
what, why, how 9–12
white lies 59
wisdom, inner 92, 97, 132
words 47–9
WorkOuts:
  1. Motivation Recharge 1–18
  2. Soul Detox 19–45
  3. Minding Your Language
    46–67
  4. The Relationship Equation
    68–90
  5. Learning to Meditate 91–117
  6. Taking the Leap and Finding
    Your Purpose 118–41
  7. Holding Your Purpose and
    Living with Joy 142–61
worry xiii, 94–5
written word 47

'yes', saying 58–60